Swimming Ponds

Frank von Berger

Swimming Ponds

Natural Pleasure in Your Garden

Type set in Zurich BT

ISBN: 978-0-7643-3433-7
Printed in China

Originally published by Verlag Georg D.W. Callwey, Munich
Translated by Dr. Edward Force

Schiffer Books are available at special discounts for bulk purchases for sales promotions or premiums. Special editions, including personalized covers, corporate imprints, and excerpts can be created in large quantities for special needs. For more information contact the publisher:

Published by Schiffer Publishing Ltd.
4880 Lower Valley Road
Atglen, PA 19310
Phone: (610) 593-1777; Fax: (610) 593-2002
E-mail: Info@schifferbooks.com

For the largest selection of fine reference books on this and related subjects, please visit our web site at
www.schifferbooks.com
We are always looking for people to write books on new and related subjects. If you have an idea for a book please contact us at the above address.

This book may be purchased from the publisher.
Include $5.00 for shipping.
Please try your bookstore first.
You may write for a free catalog.

In Europe, Schiffer books are distributed by
Bushwood Books
6 Marksbury Ave.
Kew Gardens
Surrey TW9 4JF England
Phone: 44 (0) 20 8392 8585; Fax: 44 (0) 20 8392 9876
E-mail: info@bushwoodbooks.co.uk
Website: www.bushwoodbooks.co.uk

Photo Credits
   Bahl Firm: pp. 26, 78, 79, 85 (all), 113, 121 right, 135. **Frank von Berger**: pp. 25 upper and lower right, 114 all, 116 all, 139. **Biotop Firm**: pp. 1, 10, 11, 13 upper, 14, 15 lower, 16 upper, 23, 25 upper and lower left, 28, 29, 30, 31, 35, 36, 41 upper and lower left, 42, 43, 44, 52, 53, 54, 55, 56, 62, 63, 64, 65, 66, 67, 68, 69, 71, 92, 93, 96 left, 97, 98, 99, 106, 119, 120, 132, 133, 140, 141, 15,0, 151, 152, 153; **Bohr and the Green**: p. 61; **Jens-Olaf Broksche**: p. 89; **Daldrup Firm**: pp. 45, 46, 95, 103, 111, 118; **Egli Firm**: pp. 2, 22, 75, 76, 77; **Fuchs Firm**: pp. 15 upper, 16 lower, 47, 57, 58, 59 lower, 96 right, 104 left and right, 108, 110, 112, 126, 127, 129; **Haas Firm**: pp. 81, 102,121 left; **Marion Harke**: p. 83; **Frank Hecker**: pp. 8-9, 13 lower, 128, 130 all, 131, 136 all, 137, 139, 144 all, 145, 146, 147, 148, 149; **Annette Hempfling**: pp. 12, 20; **Petra Jarosch**: pp. 17, 124, 142; **John Firm**: p. 32; **Andreas Kuehklken/Media Factory, Guetersloh**: pp. 38, 51, 87, 90; **Luetkemeyer Firm**: p. 107; **Hotel Marini**: pp. 72, 73, 74; **Niederberger & Wyl Firm**: p. 21; **Peppler Firm**: p. 16 center; **Private**: p. 59 upper; **Sallmann Firm**: pp. 100, 122; **Joerg Saenmger/Media Factory, Guetersloh**: pp. 18, 41 right, 48; **Schleitzer GmbH, Munich**: p. 40.

Contents

Foreword

I always like to visit the swimming ponds that I built with fellow fans some twenty years ago. Many of them are really splendid that can still stand out today as fine examples. The fascinating thing for me is the fact that these layouts were built then without any technical additions. And that the owners of these ponds, who can be called real pioneers, are proud of having used no artifices to support nature—neither circulation pumps nor filters nor skimmers to clean the surface.

Among pond owners, this awareness can already be found in the second generation. Perhaps this is because since childhood they have learned how well the swimming pond built by their parents functions and what qualities it offers all year round—not only in optical terms.

Again and again in recent years, books about swimming ponds have appeared, listing on many pages what technical innovations and achievements have been attained in swimming-pond building. Of course the trend goes in the direction of the technical. Clear water is the measure of all things thereby. Plants and animals are being eliminated more and more. Whereas water plants were featured at the beginning of development, they are being pushed aside more and more, and seen almost as disturbers. The less regeneration surface the better. The newest "development" is the swimming pond completely without water plants, on the principle that the more square meters of swimming area, the more economical the construction is. The technical development is going in the direction of the pool again, and we must make sure that the end result is not the conventional swimming pool.

I have frequently been asked to collaborate in publications on swimming ponds, and in looking over the concepts I was always concerned as to how technically burdensome the contents of these books were. This skepticism was naturally present too when the publishers came up with a plan for a swimming-pond book and consulted the Biotop firm. But since the proposal concerned creating a book in which technology stepped into the background and the readers were simply to be shown as many successful examples of swimming ponds as possible—from the smallest possible ponds to small lakes—and pond owners were also allowed to speak, suddenly a concept was on the table that pleased me as well as the publishers.

The book gives no recommendations for swimming-pond systems. Nor does it include any instructions for building them yourself. Rather it contains many tips and experiences from practice, which were collected in the last two decades, and with the help of which the interested party can make his own design and decide how he wants to go about turning his dream of his own swimming pond into reality. To exchange and cooperate with many swimming-pond owners, some of whom approached the subject very skeptically many years ago, and rave about them today, information with a very personal character has been gathered here. I am convinced that this book will inspire many a reader top create a small paradise for himself in his garden.

Peter Petrich
Business Manager
Biotop Landscaping GmbH

Water—The Most Natural Stuff in the World

Water gardens enjoy growing popularity in recent years. This is scarcely surprising, for the fascinating element of water has enchanted people for ages. It changes gardens into pleasantly cool, luxuriantly green refuges that promise stressed people of today recreation and relaxation from everyday life. With ponds, brooks, and water play, water can be integrated into almost any garden, regardless of its size. The variety of possible designs, though, only reveals itself when one stays open to new ideas and recognizes what potentials sleep in the use of water in a garden. The gleaming surface of a garden pond reflects not only the blue of the sky, but also the longing for a fulfilled dream.

Water Is Life

Water seems as ordinary to use as the air that we breathe. And just as we need air, we also need water to exist, for this wonderful liquid is the elixir of all life on earth.

But what is water? Simply a colorless liquid, the combination of two chemical elements, namely hydrogen (H) and oxygen (O)? Water is much more than many people think it is. It covers a large part of our planet's surface, whether in liquid or, in the polar icecaps, on the summits of high mountains, and in glaciers, in a frozen condition. Salty water forms seas and oceans, sweet water supplies brooks, rivers, lakes and ponds. It falls from the sky as rain and bubbles up out of the depths of the earth, plunges down rocky cliffs in breathtaking waterfalls, and drips from the roofs of underground caves. However and wherever we meet water, whether as quiet ponds or mighty, tearing storms, whether as endless oceans or dewdrops on a flower—water always has an irresistible fascination for people. Children are magically drawn by water, but adults also cannot escape the magic of this element. Splashing mountain streams, mirror-like ponds, and even little puddles lure us with their secrets to observe and discover. And usually it does not stop with observation: The wish for direct contact leads us only too easily to dip our hands in the water, let our feet hang in the cool wetness on a hot summer day and, if possible, plunge completely into it and seek refreshment and relaxation.

Water—Always and Everywhere

Water is everywhere and always obtainable. We use it in agriculture, in energy production, in industry and in the household. We attribute cleanliness, health and recreation to it. When we turn on the water faucet in our homes, a fresh wetness streams out, so clean that we can drink it without hesitation. We shower, bathe and swim in drinking water, we wash our laundry in it, water our gardens and flush our toilets without thinking about where this water comes from and how it was purified and distributed. It seems there is always enough of it. But that is not assured. Where the water supply is not sufficient or the technology fails to turn available water into germ-free drinking water, clean water becomes an expensive commodity.

An Expensive Commodity

In many parts of our world, for example in the extensive desert areas of Africa and Asia and on the Arabian peninsula, water cannot be taken for granted. There it rains only rarely or almost never. On the western slopes of the Atacama Desert in South America there are even regions where it has perhaps not rained for decades. Whoever is the owner of the water there also has the power, for in the dusty dry deserts water means nutrition and survival. Without water life shrivels, nothing grows in the fields, and animals die of thirst.

Water lilies are a sign of living water.

Right: *On the banks of a pond, processes of coming and going are revealed.*

Left: *Naturally pure water is also found in biologically filtered swimming ponds.*

Left page: *The heaven and the earth are mirrored in quiet water surfaces.*

Below: *Mountain streams are the embodiment of fresh, clear water.*

Underwater plants provide natural purification of water.

Naturally Pure

But also where water is available in sufficient quantities, rethinking in dealing with this elixir of life is appropriate. Instead of thoughtless waste and expensive distribution of water for use, the concept of the quality of that costly fluid becomes ever keener. How wonderfully refreshing clear water can be is realized by many only when they hike in the hills and take a sip from a fresh spring, or take a cooling dip in a lake. Many people know water almost exclusively in the form of chlorinated, biologically practically dead swimming-pool or tap water. Yet it should be perfectly natural to be able to enjoy water with all our senses, without chemical or technical preparation.

Water as a Sensual Experience

Clean water in your own garden, without chlorination or elaborate filtering technology, is thus something very special. Closeness to water can thus be produced very simply and without great technical efforts. Fountains, gravel pools, or even just a basin in the form of a watertight tub into which a small pump was sunk, give a garden or terrace a very special atmosphere with their tranquilizing bubbling. Constant maintenance of the layout is not necessary. Even artificially laid-out ponds and formal basins are almost maintenance-free, for their water is kept clean with the help of a varied and balanced planting. The calm and relaxation that radiates from such still water is of incalculable value in a world driven by progress and speed and always aimed at maximizing profit, prestige and short-term success. Such oases of rest are possible in almost any garden.

Alternative Swimming Ponds

With well-thought planning and a solid design, ponds—no matter what size—can be created after the model of nature on almost any plot of land. Such a body of water becomes even more valuable if one can also swim in it. Swimming ponds that function by the principle

Not only children enjoy play and fun in cool water.

A broad platform adjoins the shore of this swimming pond.

A pavilion by the water is a special formative element.

A bench for contemplative moments on the shore.

of self-purification and work without chemicals and technical apparatus are becoming more and more popular. They replace the cold turquoise-blue swimming pools of the economic miracle era, which can be maintained only with a high degree of care and, despite the enormous application of work and technology, allow only a very limited experience of the world of water.

Swimming ponds, on the other hand, surprise one again and again by their variety of plants and animals, the liveliness of their shores, and not least, the quality of the soft water that skin can bear especially well. And a swimming pond lives, develops like an organism, and changers constantly.

Variety Instead of Monotony

Whoever lays out a natural type of swimming pond on his property thereby takes on the responsibility for a sensible ecological system. Plants and animals are introduced or find their own way there in time. They profit from an environment that is available more and more rarely in modern times, for through increasing surface sealing, draining of wetlands and building on them, the valuable habitats of amphibians, insects, swamp and water plants, and other living things are destroyed. Laying out a natural swimming pond can thus be a contribution to breaking up the monotony of the landscape and maintaining a variety of life.

Water in the Garden:
The Dream of Your Own Pond

Water in the garden has an irresistible attraction for young and old. The reflecting surface of a pond, the mysterious green of the deep-water zones that seem to be full of life, the gentle murmur and gurgle of a stream, and the cheery splashing of bubbling water plunging over stone steps in cascades into the pond—a true delight for all who seek refreshment and relaxation in the green paradise of their own garden. Purity is also that for which all strive who occupy themselves with the idea of having their own swimming pond. Finally, the complete lack of chemical purifying apparatus and complicated clearing technology are the main reasons for the turn to natural clearing of the water.

Enjoying Pond Landscapes

Who does not dream of a natural oasis of rest in his own garden? Of stretching out, surrounded by green leaves and fragrant flowers. Taking a nap accompanied by the twitter of birds and the soft rustling of leaves in the wind. Spending an afternoon at one's own garden pond, watching the dragonflies in their artistic flight maneuvers and admiring the charm of the perfect water lilies—a luxury that more and more garden owners attain, for thanks to an ever-growing stock of completed ponds, high-quality pond foil, many accessories, plants, and also specialized advice from special firms, the dream of your own pond can be realized quite simply, even by the layman.

But the pond is finally finished, and when one no longer must miss the quiet, musing hours on the shore, perhaps new dreams arise. How wonderful it would be to be able to have a refreshing dip in a new-made garden pond on a hot summer day! To be sure, most garden ponds are only suited for cooling your bare feet; but not for realizing your wish for relaxing bathing pleasure in your own pond. So-called swimming ponds with their planted banks not only look as beautiful as natural ponds, but above and beyond that, they offer pleasant bathing in wonderfully soft water—completely without chemicals. The magic formula for the functioning of this form of your own bathing water is "nature instead of technology." For what has been done on a grand scale in nature for millions of years can also be done in a small way to keep water healthy and full of life.

The surface of the water reflects the landscape into the garden.

Swimming Ponds—Living Water in the Garden

Many swimming-pool owners are tired of constantly having to use chemical preparations and laborious, vulnerable technology to keep swimming-pool water pure. Or they may have developed skin allergies to chlorine, ozone, and other unavoidable algae killers and disinfectants in the pool, and shudder at the sight of a sterile basin of crystal-clear water, because they know that a single short dip in it must be paid for with red eyes and rashes. There are also the esthetic components: the conventional turquoise-blue pools with their conventional rectangular designs seem like foreign bodies in a garden and scarcely blend with an attractive natural garden concept.

Until about twenty years ago, though, there was practically no alternative to the system of chemical-technical water preparation with chlorine and filters if one wanted to enjoy bathing in one's own garden. But the times have changed, and more and more garden owners are deciding for the soft and natural alternative to a pool, namely a swimming pond. Since the late 1980s, at first in Austria, then in Switzerland and Germany, the first swimming ponds after nature's model have been built. After initial skepticism, this concept has been winning more and more convinced adherents, so that by now almost every third newly planned private body of swimming water is being built by this principle.

What is a Swimming Pond Anyway?

The difference between a conventional swimming pool and a swimming pond consists above all of the fact that in a swimming pond no chemical substances and, as a rule, only a few added technical installations are necessary to keep the water at a qualitatively high level with no health risk. Instead, the water is filtered and prepared by the plants around the pool. The water, fully chemical-free and safe for those with allergies, is not only splendidly fresh and clear, but also corresponds to the water quality of a natural lake. Even the planted shore resembles a lake or pond more than a swimming pool and

Swimming ponds offer untroubled fun for the whole family.

allows a perfect integration of the swimming pond into the rest of the garden.

Another advantage is that the swimming pond is in season all year long. To be sure, it is used, like a conventional swimming pool, for swimming only in the warm months, but while a swimming pool is drained of water in winter and becomes a useless, unattractive part of the garden, the swimming pond remains a living, ecologically valuable biotope that invites one to observe and admire its variety of plants and small animals, even though in winter the wind whistles through the dry reeds on the shore and spreads snow on the mirror of ice.

Build It Yourself or Not?

Deciding to build the swimming pond yourself or have it done by a specialist firm depends, among other things, on your own skill at the work, the available time, and the financial resources. But before the actual building begins, a theoretical foundation should be built. Whoever wants to gather information for the planning stage will find numerous books, newspaper articles, and internet information that will answer many questions. The available products and services for biologically purified swimming and bathing ponds have expanded notably in recent years. For example, not only tips and building instructions, but addresses and products for potential swimming-pond builders can be found on the internet, and so can complete swimming-pond kits at reasonable prices.

With all one's enthusiasm for such a broad spectrum of information, though, it should not be forgotten that one, for all these offers, stands alone and without help in the end if something goes wrong. Questions like the size of the regeneration areas, the right slope for the banks, the suitability of the substrata for the various edge zones, the choice of plants and possibly necessary clearing technology, can simply overwhelm the layman. Professional pond builders not only build on a rich fund of practical experience, but are also aware of the latest level of technology and know the innovations and products.

Errors Can Be Expensive

Building a swimming pond is, of course, not as difficult or complex as building a house, but the smooth functioning of the pond system depends on so many technical and biological combinations that an inclusive knowledge of the materials needed to carry out the project successfully is absolutely necessary. Whoever thinks he can save money by doing it alone often makes a mistake with bad results. Usually it turns out to be more expensive if one completely avoids knowledgeable, competent personal service by a professional swimming-pond builder. Resulting repairs or the removal of faults often involve just as much expenditure as completely new construction. In addition, faulty or subsequently improved swimming ponds are often only a compromise or a mere imitation of what would have been possible if a professional had done the work from the start.

Affording Your Own Work

Whoever really wants to save money by building his swimming pond can reduce the costs by his own work. It is best to speak frankly about this with the hired pond builder

Before the work begins, the specialists not only know best how a layman can usefully and safely lend a hand, but are often even glad to have constructive cooperation. In the end, well-informed builders are usually also competent swimming-pond owners because of their thorough knowledge of the methods, techniques, operating concepts and biological results involved in the pond.

The building site of a swimming pond: Much work must be done before the first plunge.

The Principle of Natural Self-Purification

Why must a swimming pond be planned carefully and surrounded by a vegetation zone? Why cannot one simply dispense with the chemical additives to swimming-pool water and leave everything to itself? What would happen to the swimming-pond water without its being cleared?

Clearing the water is necessary simply because various algae would occur after just a short time. Gnat larvae and other animals would settle in the water, a layer of mud composed of dead algae, in which water plants grow, would gradually build up. After some years the swimming pool would take on a biological balance similar to that of a natural pond—meanwhile, the swimming pool would not be usable, since the water quality would leave very much to be desired.

Biological Clearing Saves Time

Whoever would like to take the step from a pool to a more nearly natural, biologically self-cleaning swimming pond need not wait for decades until the change has come about. One can help nature along and generally bathe in splendidly fresh and clear water, usually in the year the swimming pond was built. Through the deliberate planting of numerous plants in the newly created swimming pond, the time is shortened and a biological clearing of the water becomes possible from the first hour on. In such a pond, bacteria are also part of the system, and imported germs are no problem, since they do not increase in the water and are eliminated naturally.

With so-called repositioning plants such as cattails (Typha), the water in the swimming pond is cleared naturally.

Clean Water Thanks to Plants

In a natural swimming pond there are various living areas for plants, animals and microorganisms in the variously deep shallow water zones. The motor that mixes and moves the water is the wind. Several times a day the water levels are thereby changed. The "uncleaned" water that carries floating material thus reaches the regeneration zone where the dirt particles settle to the bottom between the plants. Microorganisms (bacteria) that live there change the dirt into components of the sediment, thus to "plant food". The plants growing in this zone take up these nutrients just like other nutrients that float freely in the water and, with the help of sunlight, turn them into biomasses through photosynthesis. Thus nutrients are withdrawn from the water, and thus the algae can scarcely find food or expand their numbers explosively. As a result, the water remains clear and fresh. If the water and shore plants expend too much, they are divided and cut back. The plant parts that die off in the winter must also be removed from the water at the right time, so that the nutrients in them are not released in the process and dissolved in the water.

Clear Water is Nutrient-Poor

The natural form of water clearing by a simple clearing zone, completely without technology, functions in a properly planned swimming pond with lasting success as long as the water is consequently kept nutrient-poor. Fish "fertilize" the water with their droppings and quickly bring the sensitive circulation to a state of collapse. Too nutrient-rich substrata, in which plants are set, have a similar effect. This results, for example, through the arrival of falling autumn leaves or nutrient-rich topsoil from outside the swimming pond, such as through erosion. Drainage all around the pond helps against the latter by preventing surface water from flowing into the pond.

If the vegetation zone was planned to be big enough, the swimming-pond system can overcome changes in nutrient levels relatively problem-freely.

GOOD TO KNOW

Biological Self-Cleaning

When the subject of self-cleaning of swimming ponds comes up, this means natural self-cleaning by the repositioning plants under the water and along the shore. Cattails, pondweed, and also such attractive plants as water lilies help to keep the water quality on a high level without further help. The biologically cleared water of a swimming pond corresponds to the clear, soft water of a lake in the world of nature. Microorganisms (the so-called zooplankton) and plants in the water keep natural processes in operation through their metabolic activities. In the end they make sure that harmful germs as well as superfluous algae are permanently kept down. This occurs in the swimming pond primarily through the principle of nutrient shortage. Where algae find no nutrients they cannot exist. And if too many algae occur nevertheless, then the microorganisms make sure that after a short time the water in the swimming pond is crystal-clear again.

Plants for the Pond

Hornwort *(Ceratophyllum demersum) Snakelike shoots up to a meter long, with needle-like leaves that move freely in the pond ("underwater swimming plants). The shoots break easily into small parts that form new plants. With rich nutrients, hornwort inclines to grow wildly. Short pieces overwinter on the pond bottom, dead shoots are fished out of the water in the autumn.*

Sedge *(Carex species) Type of grasses with mostly evergreen types suitable for moist and swampy ground. Along with the decorative sedges (Carex acuta,) the false cypress grasses (C. pseudocyperus) and the shore sedges (C. riparia) are suitable for the shallow-water zone. For the shore area, the choice is among swamp sedge (C. acutiformis), yellow sedge (C. flava), morning-star sedge (C. grayi) and palm-frond sedge (C. musingu-mensis). Water depth: 5 to 10 centimeters.*

Pondweed *(Potamogeton species) Both curly (P. crispus) and floating pondweed (P. natans) have two types of leaves. The quickly spreading underwater leaves enrich the water with oxygen. Later lancet-oval floating leaves appear on the surface and shade the plant parts below. Large underwater leaves grow on showy pondweed (P. lucens). For small ponds, P. crispus is better suited. Water depth: 30 to 80 centimeters.*

Arrowleaf *(Sagittaria sagittifolia) Winter-strong plants with characteristic arrow-shaped leaves up to 25 centi-meters long and small white flowers on stems a meter high. Floating leaves up to 80 centimeters long are formed underwater. In the autumn, onion-like overwin-tering knobs appear on the ends of the stems. Water depth: 10 to 30 centimeters.*

Regeneration Zones

A variously planted clearing zone, called a regeneration zone in professional terms, and sufficient underwater plants are better for the job of clearing in any case than a zone laid out by purely optical criteria. The more varied and rich the shore zone is, the more interesting it will also be for the viewer. In the shore zone, additional niches can be created for nature, making a growth of mosses and ferns possible—for many small animals, but also for birds, a welcome resting and bathing place.

Ponds with Integrated Plant Clearing Zones

The original idea of the swimming pond is based on the harmonious unity of the swimming pool and the regeneration zone that is responsible for water purity. In this system a regeneration zone is added on one or more sides to the deep basin intended for swimming and bathing. The various depth zones in this area offer the plants needed to clear the water a suitable living space. Swimming and regeneration zones form an optical unity in ideal cases—the entire scene resembles a normal garden pond with its planted shore. Thus a swimming pond with an integrated regeneration zone can be included very well in a natural garden concept. When a new swimming pond is laid out, surface cleaning with a skimmer and the integrated clearing zone constitute the most often chosen and most problem-free type of water clearing, but additional installations such as pumps cannot always be omitted. The planted shore zone should be about as big as the swimming zone.

The regeneration zone is clearly separated from the swimming zone, so that no expanding plants disturb one's swimming pleasure.

Water Circulation

In a clearing zone integrated into a swimming pond, the high basin wall between the swimming and planted zones serves to protect the bottom of the plant area from being disturbed by swimming activity, and by not letting any substratum get into the swimming zone. For a natural impression and good water circulation between the swimming and clearing zones, it is desirable to set the basin edges as deep as possible under the water line, but high enough so that they can fulfill their restraining function.

In already existing conventional swimming pools too, a suitable new structure can form an integrated pond zone by breaking off the edges of the masonry or poured concrete basin some 30 to 40 centimeters and linking it directly with an appropriately large planted shoreline zone.

Ponds With Separate Clearing Basins

Building a swimming pond with a separated pond zone makes sense when, among other things, the topography does not allow the building of a pond with an integrated regeneration zone. For example, on a sloping plot of land or one with a problematic ground profile, a separate clearing basin can be the solution to the space problem. In existing swimming pools as well, that are to be made into swimming ponds with biological self-cleaning afterward, building a separate clearing zone is a possible alternative to rebuilding the walled swimming pool. The advantage of this solution is that no structural changes to the pool are needed, the pool character remains the same, but chemical means of cleaning can be omitted in the future. One disadvantage is the intensive use of pumps, for in all layouts with separate clearing basins, additional technology is needed. The water must be pumped from the swimming pond into the clearing basin and, after the biological clearing, pumped back in. In an ideal case, the separate clearing basin is located at the highest spot in the swimming-pond area. Then the water must only be pumped up from the swimming pond, and will flow back to the swimming pond by itself.

Functioning

The water is pumped out of the swimming pond and, after the mechanical filtering of the coarse particles, is conducted into a separate clearing basin or swamp layout for further clearing. The pumping can be done from the deepest part of the swimming zone, but it makes more sense to take the water via the skimmer that cleans the water surface of leaves and the like. A separate clearing basin can likewise be laid out like a pond, with zones of various water depths like the regeneration area of the swimming pond, with an integrated plant filter. A clearing zone consists of either one or several successive clearing stages. Clearing zones are basins made watertight with foil, arranged in steps, lined with gravel and planted with so-called repositioning plants.

In swimming ponds with integrated plant filters, the vegetation zone takes over this task. Typical repositioning plants are, for example, cattails *(Typha* species), swamp iris *(Iris pseudacorus)*, rush *(Juncus effusus,)* bur reed *(Sparganium erectum)* and calamus *(Acorus calamus)*. One must be warned that reeds form aggressive root runners that can damage the pond foil.

The water must bubble slowly through the clearing zone and is then ducted or pumped back into the swimming pond in a cleared condition. As with the integrated plant clearing setup, one reckons on about the same size for the clearing zone as for the water area of the swimming basin.

Filtering and Clearing Technology

A professionally built swimming pond with sufficient planting both under the water and in the shore area needs no added filtering even for normal swimming activity. The full lack of pond technology is for ecologically aware people one of the main reasons for building a swimming pond. Naturally dark water is also tolerated in some seasons (especially in spring). But because crystal-clear water is more and more often desired for swimming, here is some information on filters, pumps and pond technology.

Filters

If unduly large quantities of floating algae occur over a long period, the installation of a filter to clear the water is appropriate. Dark-tinted water should not be equated with bad water quality. It is only an optically disturbing factor for the user.

Two basic filter types can be distinguished, the mechanical and the biological. A combination of both systems is ideal. Pumps that suck the water out of the swimming pond and move it to the filter are required for all filter systems, and are located either in or out of the water. In

the filter, coarse particles and floating matter are removed before the water flows or is pumped back to the swimming pond. Excessive nutrients are disintegrated by bacteria. They form a bio-lawn, which removes organic dirt from the flowing water, on the corners of the filter.

Skimmers

The combination of a filter and z surface cleaner, also called a skimmer, is ideal. The skimmer, usually installed at the rim of the pond, and fitted with a leaf-catching grid, collects leaves and other coarse materials floating on the water surface before the water runs into a shaft. Here either mechanical clearing takes place or a pump moves the pre-filtered water to a mechanical or biological filter system. It is best to install the skimmer at the place on the pond rim to which the prevailing wind drives all the drifting particles. The skimmer also collects uprooted or broken-off parts of water plants from the surface. The grid must be cleaned regularly after being dirtied.

Mechanical Filter Systems

The mechanical filtering of the pond water is usually done with a multi-chambered system. After coarse filtering in the first chamber, done by brushes or foam cushions, algae are filtered out and held back in the second chamber by fine-pored foam plates or similar materials. In a further chamber, the water seeps through porous material like gravel, quartz sand, pierced bricks or stone rubble.

So-called UV filters also work mechanically in principle. The effect of UV filters is based on ultra-violet radiation, which attacks the cells of green floating algae. The result is that the algae form clumps and are more easily caught in the filter. Harmful bacteria are also reduced in this manner.

The carbonator pot is filled with a special granulate.

A brook supports the self-cleaning of the swimming pond.

Biological Filter Systems

After passing through a crude filter that removes leaves and other debris from the pond water, the water can be purified biologically in a plant filter. Aerobic bacteria that settle on the porous surface of a special stone remove organic dirt and can also remove excess nutrients from the water. The seeping must proceed very slowly so that the process works effectively. The filter material must be checked now and then and perhaps changed after some time.

An elegant solution consists of directing the cleared water back to the swimming pond through a small brook or waterfall. The filter can naturally be placed at the same place, so that less pumping energy is required.

Pumps

All pumps (except solar pumps) are run by an electric motor connected with the electric system, and are mounted externally as dry pumps in a separate pump shaft. This heightens the safety of the swimmers and makes servicing the pump easier. Immersion pumps are forbidden in swimming ponds! They can be used only when they are mounted in a separate shaft, which is not practical for reasons of cost.

For small ponds, a circulating pump ("wet runner") with a maximum capacity of 100 to 150 liters per minute can be used. In case of doubt, it is better to decide for a somewhat stronger pump, since pressure is lost in the intake and exit hoses. A disadvantageous throttling, such as by the hose being squeezed, is always possible. When buying any equipment, one should remember that the hose couplings from various manufacturers are usually incompatible. In any case, advice from a specialist dealer is necessary. One must also make sure that the pump bears a VDE, TU"V or GS seal. For reasons of safety, it is best to leave installing the pump to a specialist. If you install it yourself, all the applicable safety rules must be followed (see page 115: Safety Around the Pond).

Pump Care

Most pumps have a pre-filter. This prevents coarse particles of dirt from being sucked into the pump and clogging it. The pre-filter must be cleaned at times to keep the pump's performance constant. In winter the pump must be removed from its shaft, so that it does not freeze.

Uses of Pumps in and by the Swimming Pond:
to run filters
to supply fountains or sprays
to provide additional oxygen
to clean the pool bottom in the swimming area
to change water levels to equalize temperatures
to lower the water level for maintenance or repairs

Swimming Ponds with Foil Linings

Waterproofing the swimming pond with foil is so simple and easy that it is almost always the normal thing to do. Other waterproofing measures for pools, such as clay, covering the whole pond with waterproof concrete or using pre-formed plastic basins, can scarcely compete with modern pond foils in terms of easy application, maintenance or durability, or are not suitable for larger ponds. In any building supply store or garden shop they can be bought by the meter from a roll in various widths and thicknesses, but scarcely any swimming pond can be covered without combining foil pieces. In every case, a specialist should be called on to do this job.

The boom that garden ponds and moist biotopes have experienced in recent years has led to a clear improvement in quality for the formerly stiff, tough and yet sensitive foils. Today

Very large swimming ponds can also be integrated into the landscape and look natural, thanks to waterproof foil.

there are non-toxic, flexible, extremely durable and root-fast foils available, which give off no harmful substances to either the pond water or the surroundings and have a neutral effect on the environment.

Foil Quality

Now as before, the most useful foils are made of polyvinyl chloride (PVC). They can be sealed relatively simply with hot-air sealing devices. Foils made of polyethylene (PE) are friendlier to the environment and can also be sealed with heat. An alternative is foil of synthetic rubber (butyl), which is also very elastic, flexible and durable at low temperatures. They are also environment-friendly and can be sealed easily with a special adhesive. The disadvantage of these foils is that they are available only in black. But there are also dark green, brown and dark gray foils. Dark colors are inconspicuous, suggest optical depths and blend most naturally with shore plants. Light pond foils soon look dirty from deposited sediments and thus must be cleaned more often per year than dark foils. By now almost all foils on the market are resistant to heat, cold and UV rays.

Foil Thickness

Pond foil is available in various thicknesses between 0.5 and 2.2 millimeters. For a swimming pool, because of the high pressure caused by swimming use, but also because of the planting of the shoreline and the possible formative use of stones, a foil thickness of 1.5 millimeters is recommended. It is sufficiently firm and at the same time flexible enough. With thicker foils, one often underestimates the weight, and they are hard to work. The 1.5-millimeter foil is, to be sure, more than twice as expensive as thin foils, but the higher price is worth it in the long run, for there is nothing worse for a pond owner that a non-watertight pond. Repairing a filled, leaking pond is very laborious and costly, since the water must be pumped out, and the plants and substrate layers in the shore zone must also be removed in order to find the leak.

The Right Workmanship

Laying the foil depends on careful workmanship, so that no holes occur. Too many folds also influence the appearance. Before laying it, a careful preparation of the ground under it is essential. The excavated pond area should be free of stones and pointed or angular objects. Protection is also offered by a special textile-like fleece made of propylene, with a strength of 300 grams per square meter. This is laid under the foil and also isolated.

Cutting and laying the foil, along with gluing or sealing the joints, is a difficult job and is best done by a specialty firm in warm, dry weather, since the foil is then most flexible.

Capillary Blockage

So that the water will not be sucked up by the capillary effect of the adjoining ground, the proper working of the foil along the edge of the pond is especially important. Simply digging in the foil edges in the adjoining lawn or bed is not enough. For a capillary block, it is first laid sloping up to the ground level of the garden and then set up vertically, so that the edges of the foil rise up above the water level. For a stable capillary block, the foil is drawn over an edging of concrete blocks or plastic. Wooden planks, stone steps or blocks of stone hold the set-up foil edges.

All the work—except sealing the foil—can also be done by laymen, as long as they have sufficient skill and strength. The laborious calculation of how much foil is needed, the heavy weight of the foil, its sensitivity to damage, laying it as fold-free as possible, and particularly gluing or sealing it on the spot, though, are factors that recommend hiring a specialist firm to do the job. This is, of course, more expensive at first glance, but always pays. Unsightly folds not only influence the appearance but are also weak points at which heavy particles of dirt can gather. An expensive foil can be ruined by improper laying, which makes the job much more expensive in the end.

A swimming pond under construction shows how carefully the foil must be laid.

Swimming Ponds with Concrete Walls

Concrete is a building material that, because of its plastic qualities, is well suited in principle to pond building. Curved banks can be made more easily than with stone blocks, walls can be built quickly and surely in casting technique. The pond bottom also appears more natural than black plastic foil, since algae soon settle on the rough concrete surface. Working the material, though, is not simple and must in any case be carried out carefully so that no cracks result. When the bottom sets, hairline cracks can still form in time. Frost can also shorten the lifetime of concrete ponds. To make them watertight, pond foil has to be spread over the concrete. One should also consider that removing a concrete basin when a garden is redesigned involves a great deal of work.

Casting or Concrete Blocks

A neat division of the vegetation zone from the swimming zone can be made with a concrete wall that is built before the swimming pond is covered with pond foil. It is more stable than an earthen wall and can replace it where the ground is too soft and breaks away. Other than forms of metal or wood, concrete casting stones can be used. They are economical and easier to work with. In use, though, one has to make sure that the upper edge of the wall and the inside of the pond, where the foil contacts it, are as smooth as possible. A fleece can even out small uneven spots but not angles or corners. Through the pressure of water, they would damage the foil in time. Before covering the swimming pond with foil, one can plaster over pointed areas with mortar.

Concrete as a building material for swimming ponds can result in surprisingly attractive results, as this example shows.

From Swimming Pool to Swimming Pond

In many gardens from Economic Miracle times there are conventional swimming pools with turquoise-blue protective paint, or those that were lined with tiles. What was planned then, full of optimism, as a modern spare-time layout often developed in time into a laborious chore that required not only a lot of technical apparatus but also quite expensive chemicals in order to work. Often enough, the water was drained in a mood of resignation and the abandoned, at worst even neglected pool became an eyesore in the garden—annoyingly set in a prominent location in the middle of the lawn and very visible from all sides. Sometimes when a house was sold, such a pool even stepped surprisingly into the life of the new owner. Suddenly confronted with the question of whether to renovate the pool and equip it with the newest technology or tear it out and fill in the resulting hole (which is not cheap), more and more owners have decided for the careful rebuilding of the layout and the making of a swimming pond. The departure from the status symbol of bygone days is rewarded with a natural pond landscape, which is not only useful as a swimming place but can also become the glory of the entire garden—and all that throughout the year and costing much less than a conventional swimming pool.

Creating a Regeneration Zone

Changing a pool into a swimming pond can be done most simply by partly reforming the existing components. The essential step consists of cutting the edges of the pool down some 40 centimeters to allow the later exchange of water between the swimming and clearing zones. Around the rectangular pool, the rim of the regeneration area is then dug out to the various depths. One can also have the shore area adjoin the basin in only two or three places and use the remaining edges as an entrance zone. Depending on how the concrete basin was constructed, the former enclosure can rise up like a concrete wall in the swimming pond and separate the various zones from each other. If the regeneration zone adjoins the former basin edge, it must be made sufficiently wide to provide the plants with the necessary clearing and filtering ability. A zone must be deep enough so that underwater plants can develop. As with newly built swimming ponds, after the ground is shaped, the bottom, including the former swimming pool, is prepared with a protective layer of fleece and/or sand and then completely covered with pond foil. Such a rebuilt swimming pond functions well if the swimming zone is at least two meters deep and there is just as much room for a clearing zone as for the swimming area. In shallow basins there is the danger that the water will become too warm in summer. In any case, lowering the bottom should be considered here. A depth of two meters is often chosen so as not to stir up sediment from the bottom of the swimming area when swimming.

A Separate Clearing Basin

If one wants to combine the advantages of a swimming pond with the clean lines of a conventional pool, one can also add a separate clearing basin in which the water from the pool is regenerated by plants and then returned to the swimming basin. But in any case, this requires technical support in the form of pumps and filters, On the former finish of the pool with tiles or paint, algae inevitably settle for lack of chemical biocides. Motion of the water causes bad-looking pale, smeared spots. Alternatively, one can cover the basin with pond foil.

Swimming Ponds with Built-in Wooden Basins

Why a wall is needed as a separation between the swimming and vegetation zones has already been explained above. In many swimming ponds this wall is made of the existing terrain or built of concrete before the waterproofing foil is laid on the pond bottom. Alternatively, the swimming basin can also be bordered with the help of a wooden structure built on the already laid pond foil. The advantage of a wooden separation is mainly the optical charm that the natural material affords. Wooden basins are especially good for small layouts, like diving basins in sauna gardens, or those that offer summertime refreshment. Wading pools for children can also be separated nicely from the vegetation area with wooden basins. Additions like ladders, stairs or steps can be included in the wooden basin easily and harmoniously. If one does not have a great deal of experience, time and woodworking skill, one does best to hire a carpenter to do the building. With the cost of the materials, and especially for the many hours of work, a large wooden basin for as real swimming pond unfortunately becomes very expensive. The price of a swimming pond with a wooden basin can easily be double that of a normal foil pond.

Planning and Building

Native larch wood is best suited for use by and under water. It is also long-lived and stable without impregnation. Whether so-called "moon wood"—wood that comes from trees that were felled in certain phases of the moon—really have better quality and a longer life than "normal" wood has not been proved scientifically to date. The decision is thus left up to the individual.

The wooden basin must be built very carefully, for it is placed on the already laid-out, sensitive pond foil. A layer of protective fleece between the wooden parts and the foil is absolutely necessary so that the latter is not damaged by splinters, sharp angles or corners. To stabilize the basin, angled braces (reaching into the vegetation zone) are installed on the back and attached to a horizontal beam on the pond bed. The upper edge of the basin, some 40 to 50 centimeters below the water level, is formed with wide planed and smoothed boards that can also serve as underwater seats for bathing fun. So the wooden structure does not float, it has to be weighted down with strewn gravel.

Diving Basins with Ecological Clearing

After sweating in a sauna or on a hot, sticky summer day, it is very refreshing to cool off in a diving basin in the garden. One does not have to install a large layout, for this is not a place for swimming, but only for a quick immersion and spontaneous cooling. The basin need be only deep enough so that one can immerse oneself completely in the cooling liquid. Instead of a conventional diving basin filled with tap water and cleared by chemical and technical means, this can also be done in a small natural basin that functions by the principle of the self-cleaning swimming pond.

Building a naturally cleared diving basin is just like building a big swimming basin. The excavated basin and the shore zone are covered with fleece and foil, and a capillary block is installed. But since the walls of the actual diving basin are more abrupt and steep than those of a swimming pond, a supporting concrete wall or built-in wooden basin is recommended for stability. The clearing zone must have about twice as much surface area as the diving basin so it can do its job. Varying water depths of the edge, between zero and 80 centimeters, allow a varied planting with underwater, floating and shore plants that provide sufficient clearing of the water. When the diving basin has a depth between 150 and 180 centimeters and a surface of some two square meters, the water in it remains sufficiently cool, even in summer, to prevent inversion of the water. An edge running all around the edge of the basin under water, made of larch wood and serving as a seat bench, and an entrance with a ladder the leads into the water make bathing pleasure ideal. Such natural diving basins that work without any technical support and are almost maintenance-free, are especially suitable for garden spots that are outside developments and have no connection with a stream. To support turning over the water, installing a skimmer is recommended. Since only modest pump performance is needed, a solar pump can be installed. Of course here too, for safety's sake, a fence should prevent uninvited guests from wandering into the basin and being harmed.

Water Analysis

In the planning stage, but in any case before construction, the filling water should be tested for suitability. A drinking-water analysis, such as is available in many communities, is not sufficient. The nutrient content in particular must be tested and—according to the results—the water must be prepared before filling. The testing can be done only by a specialist firm, which can then recommend the required measures. Since many of these measures also involve building requirements—such as, for example, the installation of a filling-water filter—adding such facilities later is more expensive than planning the new construction. Many problems with swimming ponds are brought on by neglecting the water analysis.

Testing the water for later analysis is done in the swimming zone.

How Much Technology is Necessary?

The principle of the self-cleaning swimming pond is based on the optimal use of the natural self-cleaning effects. Through completely natural biological, physical and chemical processes a water quality is attained that is suitable for bathing and guarantees skin-friendly water.

But despite thorough planning, it can occur that the biological clearing of the pond water does not function satisfactorily. If the water is strongly darkened by floating algae, it can become necessary to filter the water additionally. Both mechanical and biological filter systems are suitable for this. For the additional filtering, a pump has to be installed to move the water into the filter and then back to the pond.

The question of air pumps to enrich the water with oxygen often arises. But with proper planning, such installations are not necessary.

Sucking Out Deposits

Coarse particles floating on the water, such as blown-in leaves, can be removed from the pond surface by an automatic skimmer. From the skimmer, the water runs back into the pond, or it can be pumped into an external filter system.

After about a year, a fine sediment forms on the bottom of the swimming zone and is stirred up by swimming. This layer of sediment must be removed by a special mud sucker.

Various manufacturers offer so-called biological means of pond care. Their necessity and use are debated by swimming-pond owners. In a well-planned swimming pond with a functioning biological circulation, they really should be superfluous.

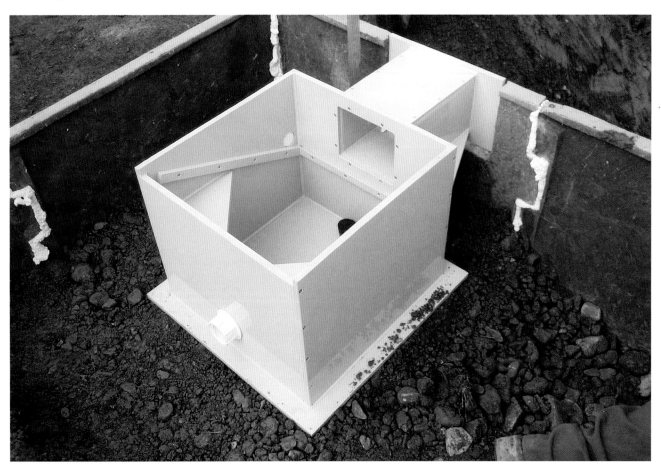

Skimmers and pumps must always be installed in a separate pump shaft.

Check List—Planning a Swimming Pond

Needed Space: The swimming area requires half the water surface; the other half is taken up by the regeneration area, perhaps with a plant filter. If desired (such as in especially steep terrain), the two areas can be laid out separately, which makes the use of technology necessary. When planning a swimming pond, consider what is to be done with the excavated soil after the pit has been dug.

Pond Size: As when building a house, the contractors tend toward a much too large water surface in the beginning. The desire to swim a long way without turning must be made relative to the number of good swimming days in your summer. The most saving can be made by reducing the water area.

Building It Yourself: Do only the jobs that you can really master. For foil sealing, consider too that devices offered in the building trade are not suitable for large operations, since they do not reach the necessary sealing temperatures. Repairing a pond usually costs more than what you spent to build it.

Signing a Contract: The most important criterion after the price and capable planning is checking references and talking with pond owners when you choose a contractor.

Technology: The more technology, the greater the danger of technical failure. The pipes should be kept as short as possible, and the pump shaft should be near the pond. As a rule, all technical operations can be driven by a pump.

Building Time: There is no ideal building time. Winter is ruled out; the weather is generally ideal in spring and early summer, but the demand is greatest, since every prospective pond owner wants to swim in the summer. Building in summer has the disadvantage of a messed-up garden at the time when one enjoys it most. Building in autumn has the advantage that the regeneration area is already developed when the next swimming season begins.

Planning and Duration: Complete planning is possible in four weeks. Delays in starting the building can be caused by obtaining necessary permits (which differs greatly from region to region), and should be inquired about at the beginning of planning. A pond of about 100 square meters can be built in about three weeks. In no case should planning be begun after excavation. Any revision of the excavation is usually very costly.

Fish: A swimming pond is a swimming pond. A fish pond is a fish pond. The requirements for the two types of well-functioning ponds are too different to combine them into one pond. Simply avoid trying!

Algae: They are components of a natural swimming pond. But excessive algae growth can become a problem. It is minimized by professionally built pond systems and supported by technical features.

Swimming-Pond Depth: As a rule, this amounts to two meters. This depth prevents sediment that sinks to the bottom from being stirred up by swimming and the water temperature from rising too far, which promotes algae growth.

Safety for Children: No fence and no warning system can replace parental responsibility. This applies to pond owners and visitors alike.

Location: The swimming pond needs as sunny a location as possible. But shading from late morning to midafternoon prevents excessive warming of the water and the fast algae growth that results. High deciduous and coniferous trees have no place in the immediate vicinity of a swimming pond. They shade the water needlessly, and in autumn their falling leaves mess up the pond water excessively.

Documentation: If cables are laid, a plan must be made during the building phase, so that no lines are damaged by later digging. Pond-building firms must provide such a plan without being asked to.

Realized Dreams

For more than twenty years, imaginative and successful swimming ponds have been built and enjoyed enthusiastically by their owners. But since the ponds are often used quietly and the bathing pleasure is usually shared only with the family and closest friends, one usually hears nothing, or only by roundabout routes, of the experiences that the owners have had with their ponds. Such reports of everyday use, enriched with descriptions of special experiences, are often much more informative than any theories, and can offer valuable encouragement and tips to future swimming-pond users.

Variety of a Principle

The layouts often differ greatly. There is the swimming pond, which is nothing more than a small bathing basin behind the house that provides cooling in summer and a place for the children to splash happily. But there is also the extended water landscape with a swimming area several meters deep, a shallow-water basin and a fountain in the regeneration zone. And whoever believes that natural romance holds first place in the subject of swimming ponds is deluding himself: An elegantly styled designer pond can mirror the gleaming steel structure in the glass façade of the functional dwelling house and still include biological water clearing.

But now as before, there is also the naturally designed, romantic swimming pond with water lilies between rustling rushes, inviting children and adults on expeditions into the animal kingdom on the shore.

Shared Experiences

As different and individual the concepts of one's own swimming pond are, some aspects concerning maintenance and care are almost always experienced in common. In a poll of swimming-pond owners, their experience with operation, everyday care and cleaning the nearly natural swimming area could be gained

A bathing cabin sheltered from curious looks—here the dream of spare-time paradise was realized.

and drawn on for this book. These experience reports are also very important because every new swimming pond looks beautiful, but only time shows what decisions made in building it have proved themselves and which had to be revised. Things do not always function as planned, and it would not be honest to conceal the fact that one or another swimming-pond owner has installed additional technical apparatus after some years to decrease the growth of algae and improve the water quality. Other swimming-pond owners report the principle of natural self-cleaning in their pond works as expected and the system itself is operating without problems after many years of constant use.

A Piece of Your Own Life

The request for owners' very personal experiences and feelings that link them with the swimming pond in their own garden lends color and personality to their portrayals. Someone who previously took scarcely a look at insects, amphibians or other pond owners, suddenly takes and interest in the flora and fauna on the shore of his pond. Many a restless spirit who was constantly caught up in activities suddenly finds rest and relaxation at the pond, and enjoys life without any constant stress. And many simply have discovered the joys of bathing in naturally soft water, and enjoy the hours at and in the swimming pond alone or with family, friends and acquaintances.

Swimming Pleasure in the Smallest Space

The idea of building a swimming pond was nothing completely new for the owner of this jewel, for the builder's sister already had one like it. Based on this example, the future swimming-pond owners could let the pond's atmosphere inspire them and convince them that such a natural body of still water looks great all year. They were also fascinated by the fauna that made their homes by the pond, and the possibility of using the frozen surface of the pond for ice skating in winter. They still had doubts as to the size of swimming pond, for there was relatively little space available in the garden behind the house. But a firm that specialized in building swimming ponds could assure them, based on years of experience, that smaller ponds can also have functioning natural self-cleaning.

Below: *Crystal-clear, refreshing water invites an expedition into the cooling fluid.*

A Bathing Pond in a Small Garden

The garden foreseen as the home of a swimming pond is just ten meters wide, but very long—a typical "handkerchief garden", such as one often finds in our thickly settled cities. The somewhat problematic beginning situation was mastered splendidly by placing an artificial spring right beside the terrace that bordered on the house. Its water flows bubbling next to the wide steps that lead to the somewhat lower swimming pond, and into the pond. This fills almost the entire width of the property. Only on the edges are there narrow paths that lead to the back part of the garden and ease the care of the pond flowers on the shores.

Water Circulation for Fresh Water

The swimming pond is built in an angular style and includes a water-changing setup, which is very worthwhile in small-size ponds. The water circulation, which along with the planted clearing zone provides constantly clear swimming water, begins with the skimmer, which automatically cleans the water surface by removing crude particles like fallen leaves and the like. From there the water passes through a pump to the small brook near the stairs, from which the fresh water flows back into the pond. In the morning the sun shines on the water surface and warms it to a pleasant swimming temperature. The wooden walkways around two sides of it are also warmed by the sun almost all day and invite one to relax and enjoy life.

Right: *The long, narrow yard was used optimally for the building of the swimming pond. Only a narrow path remains between the pond and the wooden fence that borders the neighbors' yard.*

A look from above at the swimming pond and the nicely growing clearing zone beside it.

Older Ponds Need More Care

The pond has fully met the owners' expectations. To date they have never had to change the water and have been able to clean it of sediment once a year without problems by using the suction device attached to the pond pump. After eight years of steady use, more care will probably have to be devoted to the pond in the future, since the plants are beginning to spread and have to be cut back more often. Removing sediment from the swimming area will also have to be done more than once a year so that swimming will remain an untroubled pleasure.

Fun for the Whole Family

Now as before, the pond provides pleasure for the whole family. When it was built, the children were six and nine years old. "At that time they had great fun hurrying from the living room across the terrace into the pond," their mother reports. But as they grew older, they would have preferred a larger swimming basin in which they could swim a long way instead of splashing around. "For us that is no problem—now the pond belongs to us adults! We enjoy it particularly in the spring, observing the tadpoles, water striders and salamanders that have settled with us." The artificial brook course is a special enrichment. "It conjures up a mountain stream atmosphere and is also a big help against neighborhood noise," says the owner's wife.

Data and Facts

Year Built:
1997

Water area:
Swimming area: 21 square meters
Regeneration area: 21 square meters
Total: 42 square meters

Water depth:
2.0 meters

Technical Equipment:
Water circulation
One skimmer

Formative Elements:
Artificially laid-out brook course

Planning and Building:
Biotop Landscaping GmbH,
A-3411 Weidling

Living by the Water

A splendid plot of land with ideal prerequisites for building a swimming pond: The property, of 12,000 square meters, secluded in the rural part of Westphalia, lies three kilometers away from the nearest village. Country idylls and heavenly rest are thus guaranteed. Although there is already a large natural pond on the property, the owners still wanted a swimming pond. Because of the muddy soil, the always-muddy water and the many animals living in the water, nobody had wanted to swim in the natural lake, covering almost 1200 square meters, for many years. In addition, the natural pond lies in the rear part of the property, some distance from the house. Thus the owners decided to build the newly planned swimming pond right near the house, so as to brighten up their days with the closeness to the water. A garden-building firm in the region, that specialized in building swimming ponds, took on the planning and also carried out the work.

A Mediterranean atmosphere at the house door need not remain a dream.

Friendly Swimming landscape

Today one goes from the often-visited winter garden across a wide wooden deck directly to the shore of the big swimming pond. The dream of living by the water has become reality. From the winter garden, one's gaze sweeps across the wooden deck and over the adjacent vegetation zone that provides natural clearing of the pond water. It is separated from the swimming area by a curving wall. The long swimming zone of the pond turns to an almost round basin on one of the short sides, making turning easier for swimmers. The light green pond foil and clear water awaken an impression of friendly freshness and invite one, especially on hot summer days, to enjoy the cool, shimmering liquid—what a contrast with the dark, silted water of the old natural pond!

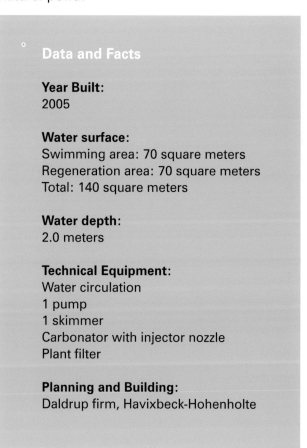

Data and Facts

Year Built:
2005

Water surface:
Swimming area: 70 square meters
Regeneration area: 70 square meters
Total: 140 square meters

Water depth:
2.0 meters

Technical Equipment:
Water circulation
1 pump
1 skimmer
Carbonator with injector nozzle
Plant filter

Planning and Building:
Daldrup firm, Havixbeck-Hohenholte

Curving Lines

Splendidly developed, exotic potted plants and small pyramidal, trimmed evergreen shrubs line the banks of the pond landscape and the nearby paths. On the shore opposite the house, an additional sitting place was attached to a wooden deck, where lounges are ready for sunbathing. Lovely solitary trees and flowerbeds form a green frame for the swimming paradise, which is framed by lawns and narrow beds planted with shrubs and slim bamboo. Individual large boulders set accents between gravel and lawn surfaces that adjoin the edges of the pond. The curving lines of the pond landscape are continued in the large surrounding park setting, and the path courses and landscape modeling blend harmoniously with the curving lines.

A large swimming area characterizes this layout, which blends harmoniously into the garden scene.

Water Landscape Instead of Decorative Garden

The owner of this swimming pond had always dreamed of living right by the water. But the property is right in the middle of a residential area in the outskirts of Munich, far away from the shore of a lake. With the completely new layout of a garden came the chance at last to fulfill the long-cherished wish. From an article about especially successful garden formations, in which a project with a swimming pond was portrayed, the builder got the idea of such a water garden. Instead of a lawn, flowerbeds and shrubs there arose, in collaboration with a firm that specialized in building swimming ponds, a pure water garden without lawns, in which the swimming pond played the central role. The two-meter-deep swimming zone is separated from the regeneration area by a wall reaching to barely under the water surface. Optically, a long deck of larch wood separates the swimming zone from the bordering gravel areas. At the end of the long lot, a spacious wooden deck offers enough space for pleasant sitting right by the water. A loose row of trees planted in cooperation with the neighbors closes off the yard and offers plenty of privacy without becoming dark or gloomy.

Bamboo and Gravel

In the regeneration area, typical regeneration plants grow, and on the adjoining gravel areas there are low flowerbeds that create colorful accents with their blossoms in the summer. But above all, nests of bamboo scattered over the entire yard create a year-long green coulisse with their attractive leafage. This is also needed, for the owner exults: "We have breakfast outdoors three quarters of the year, right by the water!" Through the loose combination of plantings and gravel areas, completely avoiding a conventional layout with beds, edges and lawns, there arose a harmonious, happy landscape that not only looks wonderful but also saves a lot of gardening work.

Sucking Instead of Mowing

Instead of regular lawnmowing, constant weeding and rose cutting, the care is concentrated on the swimming area of the pond. About four times a year, the pond bottom is cleaned of mud and sediment by a special sucking device. At the same time, the walls are brushed so that no algae settle on them. This cleaning action takes about three hours each time—"clearly less than mowing the grass every two weeks," the owner assures.

From the wooden platform in the rear part of the garden, a wide wooden stairway offers easy access to the swimming pond.

Left: *In this case the swimming pond and regeneration zones take up almost the entire lot. An attractive pond landscape has been created, with various types of sitting places, each of which offers a different view of the water.*

The reward for this work is year-round crystal-clear water that stays almost completely free of algae without using chemicals. The care of the regeneration area also stays within limits. In the spring, the dry stalks of cattails and other water plants are cut back. Since the pond is still relatively young, scarcely any other work is needed. When the plants have settled well later, the garden shears will probably have more work to do.

Professional Planning Pays

For the owners, the swimming pond has meanwhile become a firm component of their lives. It provides a vacation atmosphere almost all year, and is "the best investment that applies to our house," as the owner enthusiastically expresses it. That the result of rebuilding the garden succeeded so well and the water clearing functions completely without chemicals result above all from good planning by an experienced team. For this reason the proud pond proprietor advises all future pond owners absolutely to work together with a firm that specializes in building swimming ponds and has the required know-how.

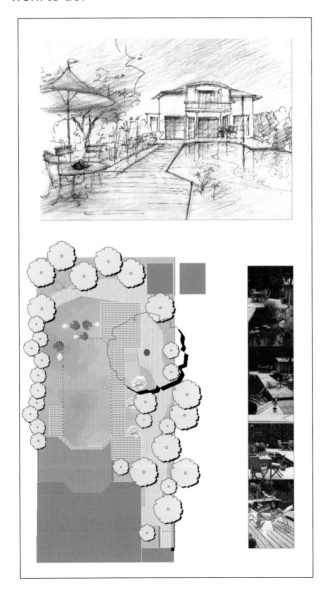

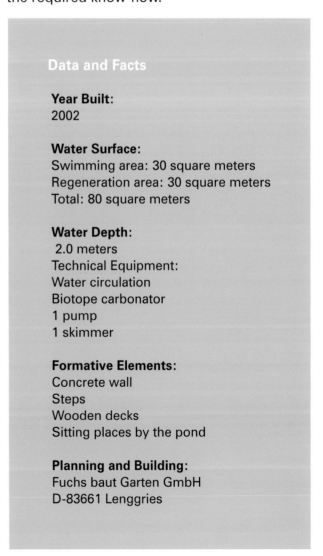

Data and Facts

Year Built:
2002

Water Surface:
Swimming area: 30 square meters
Regeneration area: 30 square meters
Total: 80 square meters

Water Depth:
 2.0 meters
Technical Equipment:
Water circulation
Biotope carbonator
1 pump
1 skimmer

Formative Elements:
Concrete wall
Steps
Wooden decks
Sitting places by the pond

Planning and Building:
Fuchs baut Garten GmbH
D-83661 Lenggries

A Diving Pond Amid Exclusive Plants

This small swimming pond owes its existence to a courageous decision. The garden of some 500 square meters is just a part of a property measuring some 2000 square meters. For a long time the owners had a plan to develop this part of the yard. But at first nothing happened for a number of years, and the garden lay asleep like the Sleeping Beauty. Finally the building plans gave way to the wish to expand the already existing garden and provide more room for life in the green world. There ensued a basic new formation of the closed-off garden area, in which a small swimming pond was on the owners' want list.

Fed by the Brook

The steeply sloping terrain is divided into two garden levels that are connected by stairs of natural stone and an artificial brook course. The brook is fed by a small pond on the upper garden level. Utilizing the natural slope, the water flows in a stream bed of broken granite slabs and empties into the small rectangular swimming pond. A platform of larch wood running around the basin separates the vegetation zone from the swimming area and serves as a place to sit. The pond, because of its small size, is less suitable for swimming than for pleasant bathing and splashing. With its larch deck it now forms the center of the garden.

Perennials and Grasses

The garden is accessible by stepping stones of gray and cream-colored granite that line up casually to form walkways. A small patch of lawn and a blockhouse to house garden tools and furniture complete the oasis of good feeling. Special emphasis was placed on planting the regeneration area by the pond and the rest of the garden. A bright table dogwood *(Cornus controversa)* shades the sitting place by the pond. Genuine Tuscan cypresses *(Cupressus sempervirens)* give the garden a Mediterranean flair. Isolated beds and grasses give the garden effective accents: Eulalia *(Miscanthus sinensis* 'Malepartus') and Siberian iris *(Iris sibirica* "Silver Edge") suit the water garden just as well as dwarf day-lily hybrids *(Hemerocallis* 'Stella d'Oro') and Japanese sedge *(Carex morrowii).*

Data and Facts

Year Built:
1999

Water Surface:
Swimming area: 9 square meters
Regeneration area: 40 square meters
Total: 49 square meters

Water depth:
2.0 meters

Technical Equipment:
Swimming area separation prepared with stainless steel wall modules
3 circulation pumps, skimmer, spring element
2 underwater radiators

Formative Elements:
Granite step plates
Steps and deck of larch wood
Brook course

Planning and Building:
Garten- und Landschaftsbau Pohl GmbH
D-93497 Willmering

Right: *A small swimming pond for refreshing in a carefully planned garden landscape.*

A Swimming Pond Purely for City People

For some twenty years this swimming pool has been pleasing its owners. At that time the concept of a swimming pond that regenerated itself biologically was still relatively new, and the owners, deciding to build a swimming basin, located a firm, quite by chance, that had specialized in building swimming ponds. One of the reasons for the biological alternative to a conventional swimming pool was the avoidance of technical and thus fragile equipment like pumps, sucking and circulating apparatus (the pond, now as then, works completely without support technology). And the fact that "mixing poisons" with chlorine tablets and other pool chemicals could be avoided made the decision for the swimming pond easier; it was also less costly to build at that time than a swimming pool. But above all, the esthetic factor played a role: The pond blends into the garden better than a conventional pool and is beautiful all year. In winter in particular, it remains attractive and is not just "a dirty, useless hole", as the owner's wife put it.

Velvet-soft Water

Through all the years, the pond has fulfilled all its owners' hopes without causing major problems. The originally feared plague of stinging gnats die not happen, and there were no algae problems worth noting. In the spring, when the plants in the regeneration area are not yet big enough to keep the nutrient content in balance through their activity, more algae sometimes build up. But they are easy to remove, and by early summer at the latest, the water is naturally clear again. Although some visitors refuse to bathe in a natural swimming pond, saying, "I prefer the blue water of a chlorinated pool," the owners use the swimming pond enthusiastically. "The water feels like velvet on our skin," the lady of the house exults. The children who have now grown and left the nest also come on hot summer days for a refreshing dip in the parental swimming pond.

A dry wall holds up the slope to the house. At the same time, it affords a protected sitting place at the pond that catches the sun's last rays in the evening.

This swimming pond was made to fit into a slight slope. Surrounding willows and nearby woods form a peaceful background.

Problem-free Thanks to Good Maintenance

The owners attribute the fact that the swimming pond has functioned so problem-free to this day to their regular maintenance. During the season, leaves and other crude particles that fall into the pond are carefully fished out, and in autumn the plants in the regeneration area are cut back. The owner's wife stresses that she understands that better than gardening and worse than special pool care, for other beds also require a certain amount of gardening attention. For the "basic cleaning" of the swimming area, a firm is hired once a year to suck out the mud and clean the walls and bottom.

Animal Guests in the Pond

The owners, who do not think of themselves as "green" people especially close to nature, but rather as normal city dwellers with very limited awareness of the environment, love their swimming pond because there is so much there to see and experience. The idyllic setting right near woods and meadows lets deer come to the pond. Observing nature by and in the water gives the whole family great pleasure. They follow with great interest the development of frog and toad eggs in the spring, from fertilization to the hatching of tadpoles and their growth into frogs. Because the swimming pond is more or less a natural body of water, there are,

in addition to frogs, dragonflies, bathing birds and all kinds of nice water snails, plus guests that are less welcome. "Not every swimmer is fascinated if he meets insect larvae, backswimmers and water beetles while swimming," the owner's wife reminds all who have the idea of building their own swimming pond. But despite the ambivalent variety, she is a great fan of the swimming-pond idea, and every spring she can even greet a pair of wild ducks that regularly try to build a nest there. But since the feathered pair make too much of a mess in raising their brood, stir up mud and disturb the whole scene, they must unfortunately be chased out again and again. "Well, they also know where would be a nice place to live," she says.

A look and the clearing zone. Among others, cattails, various types of swamp iris and water lilies have taken over the regeneration area.

Data and Facts

Year Built:
1989

Water Surface:
Swimming area: 32 square meters
Regeneration area: 32 square meters
Total: 64 square meters

Water Depth:
2.0 meters

Border between swimming and regeneration areas:
Concrete wall

Technical equipment:
None

Formative Elements:
Wooden steps
Dry wall
Artificial brook course

Planning and Building:
Biotop Landschaftsgestaltung GmbH
A-3411 Weidling

Steps and wooden decks invite one to sunbathe after swimming. The attractive plants on the edges of the pool make this a paradise of pleasure.

Swimming Pleasure for the Whole Family

Some years ago, when the owners considered building a swimming pool in their garden, they happened to find information about swimming ponds with biological water clearing. They were immediately fascinated by the much better appearance of such a layout: a body of water for swimming, with planted shores, fitting harmoniously into the garden and not looking like a foreign body—that was the alternative to a conventional pool! Before they decided on a particular firm to carry out the construction, the prospective swimming-pond owners gathered information from several specialist firms. Finally they chose a firm from there own area that already had years of experience with the building and maintenance of swimming ponds.

Experience Pays

Their search paid off, for the finished pond no only fulfilled the owners' expectations but even exceeded them, as they sincerely assure us. The whole family, and naturally their children's many friends as well, enjoy carefree days at the swimming pond. In nice weather there is always something going on there. "With it we made our dream of life by the water come true!" Thus the owner advises all future pond builders: "Be sure to hire a firm with a lot of experience, even if it is somewhat more expensive!" That guarantees trouble-free functioning and avoids burdensome repairmen when faults show up after the building. The care of the swimming [p. 56] is done by the owner himself. "How much time that takes I cannot say for sure—half a day every few weeks, perhaps. But it is fun—much more that messing around with some chemicals."

High Spare-Time Value

This large-scale swimming pond, taking up a hundred square meters including the regeneration zone, has several wooden decks on the shore that lead to the water and into the swimming zone, plus a graveled area with large chunks of rock and smoothed round stones; lightly planted, it creates a nice link with the garden. The soil dug out when the pond was built was used to build up the grounds, and the slope was held by a dry wall that goes well with the old natural stone wall at the edge of the garden. The mowed lawn between the dry wall and the pond offers enough space for a table and chairs for eating a meal outdoors, or for comfortable lounges for sunbathing.

For the owners of this swimming pond, it was especially important for the children of the family to be able to discover nature's secrets and play with no problems.

The Secret of the Salamanders

On the pond shore, between the cattails and the swamp iris, there is much for the owner to discover. The ex-city people found it fascinating that in a short time the pond became living space for countless animals. And many a riddle is not yet solved by the proprietors: "With great pleasure we discovered our first salamanders—I still think of them to this day, wondering how they could have immigrated to us."

Data and Facts

Year Built:
2003

Water Surface:
Swimming area: 44 square meters
Regeneration area: 56 square meters
Total: 100 square meters

Water depth:
2.0 meters

Technical Equipment:
Water circulation
Biotope carbonators
1 skimmer
Plant filter

Formative Elements:
Wooden decks on the shore
Gravel area
Dry wall

Planning and Building:
Biotop Landschaftsgestaltung GmbH
A-3411 Weidling

From Backyard Garden to Swimming Place

The Swimming Pond is by the House, the Clearing Area "on the Hill"

Even on sloping land that is very hard to build on, shoved in between the house and the slope, swimming ponds can be built. The best proof is this prize-winner in Upper Bavaria; from the magazine "Schoener Wohnen". Here an unused, shaded back-yard garden was turned into a swimming place of high value by building a swimming pond.

The original situation had a not very attractive back yard between the house, garage and steep slope; in the back yard there were even a meadow and a vegetable garden on the adjoining elevated garden area. The owner had wanted a water motif in the garden for a long time, preferably a pond landscape abutting directly on the terrace. At first she did not know how and, above all, where a pond could be built in the problematic topography of her garden. At a fair she then saw a swimming pond that a professional garden-building firm was displaying. The concept interested her, she asked numerous questions, all of which were answered convincingly—"and then everything happened quite fast", the owner relates. "When I saw that combining it with a natural swimming pond was possible, the decision was very clear." The meadow on the high ground and the small vegetable garden were to stay, but the entire lower garden was to be changed into a harmonious and playful swimming landscape.

The Building Phase

The building time took three months in all. The complicated situation of the yard demanded laborious logistics, every chunk of stone had to be carried singly into the garden. The excavators brought the future owner doubts for a time: "When the pit for the pond was dug, I stood up there in the evening, looked down and asked myself: "What are you doing?" I thought I had made the greatest mistake of my life. But then I did not regret it, and I never will. It was a good decision." The original concept, with minor changes, was applied as it had been planned from the start, and the pond completely corresponds to the expectations.

A Separate Clearing Basin

The swimming area, measuring some eight by five meters, and some two meters deep, is completed by a loosely planted, partly graveled shore zone and a clearing zone 1.70 meters higher. The water is pumped up from the pond and cleared biologically in the planted regeneration basin. Then it flows back into the pond through a stream course made of gravel and rock rubble from the Isar River. Steps, the terrace bordering the terrace, [p. 58] and a second sitting place somewhat higher up, are built of weather-resistant larch wood. The steep slope is held by limestone blocks. Wooden steps lead to the high meadow, which was not included in the redesigning.

Site Plan

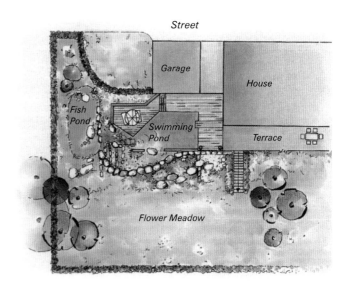

Over an artificial stream course the cleared pond water gurgles from the raised clearing zone back to the swimming pond. It covers the last meter over a projecting stone and accompanies every rendezvous on the raised sitting place with its soft splashing.

The Pond as a Thermos Bottle

Thanks to the clever pond-building technique and good maintenance, there have been no problems to date. The water is as clear as glass, and stinging gnats have stayed away. The swimming season, as a rule, lasts from May to September. Since evenings in the Upper Bavarian climate can become quite cool even in summer, the owner is especially happy with the heat-storing water surface right by the terrace. So many a summer evening is spent outside thanks to this "thermos bottle". And the water garden is used in winter as well: "At times when it is really nice, we often sit on the terrace in the winter too. And as soon as the weather is somewhat suitable in the spring, we are almost always in the garden. Our whole life takes place out here on the terrace."

Data and Facts

Year Built:
1998

Water Surface:
Swimming area: 40 square meters
Regeneration area: 40 square meters
Total: 80 square meters

Water Depth:
2.0 meters

Border between Swimming and Regeneration Areas:
Swimming and clearing zones on two levels

Technical Equipment:
1 pump
1 skimmer
Separate clearing basin

Formative Elements:
Steps of larch wood
Raised sitting place right by the water
Gravel field
Artificial stream course
Dry wall

Planning and Building:
Fuchs baut Gaerten GmbH
D-83661 Lenggries

The yard before the revision: On two sides, steep slopes limit a small, partly shaded lawn; the two other sides of the courtyard are limited by buildings.

After the revision a striking swimming pond invites one to a refreshing dip, and large sun terraces on two different levels invite relaxation.

59

Rescued Landscape

This garden of some 900 square meters originally consisted of a large lawn with a few trees. But the owners wanted the element of water to play a major role in the garden. A swimming pond, combined with a sauna house, seemed to be a promising possibility in fulfilling their wish for a water garden and simultaneously increasing the useful value of the garden. In building the swimming pond, the spoil was therefore used to even out the terrain.

Spare-Time Setup with a Long View

The avant-garde sauna house and the swimming pond are not directly linked with the house, but lie on the border of the property near a lawn. But its unique structure and glowing orange-red paint make the sauna house a striking eye-catcher in the back part of the garden. The spare-time setup is completed by a separate grille site in the farthest corner of the property. A border of robust trees, easy to care for, encloses the lot on two sides, and a hedge of hornbeam also provides for privacy. Yet the view, influenced by the slightly hilly topography of the surroundings, can sweep over the adjacent fields and meadows. The green coulisse was more or less included in the planning as a "rescued landscape" and forms a vivid background for the newly arisen spare-time area. The sauna house at the head of the swimming pond stands on a terrace of weather-resistant bangkira wood. After taking a sauna, one can first cool off in the swimming pond and then relax in a lounge on the wooden terrace. Next to the pond a walnut tree was planted, a striking solitary sign that gives a distinct accent to the otherwise open garden and provides pleasant shade in the summer.

Left: *The sauna house at the pond is the ideal place to recover from hectic everyday life.*

Year-Round Spare-Time Paradise

The swimming pond has an almost long-rectangular shape, with the shores of the regeneration zone laid out in curves and thus relaxing the strict geometry of the sauna house. A wall of mescalith stones and a broad strip of gravel separate the shore zone from the lawn. Stepping stones in the shallow water of the regeneration zone, planted with cattails *(Typha)*, water mint *(Mentha aquatuica)* and yellow swamp iris *(Iris pseudacorus)* make it possible to reach the swimming zone from the lawn. By building the swimming pond and the sauna house, the former monotony of the garden was broken.

Data and Facts

Year Built:
2002

Water Surface:
Swimming area: 48 square meters
Regeneration area: 31 square meters
Plant filter: 25 square meters
Total: 104 square meters

Water depth:
2.0 meters

Technical Equipment:
1 pump
1 skimmer

Formative Elements:
Deck of bangkira wood
Sauna house, stepping stones in the water

Planning and Building:
Bohr und das Gruen
D-66663, Merzig-Schewmlingen

Swimming Despite Building Site

How a Natural Swimming Pond was made of a Designer Pool

Many an idea matures slowly and reacts to the changes that result from conditions. The owner of this swimming pond, a businessman from Vienna, added a transparent structure of glass and wood to the garden side of the existing house. From here there was to be a free view of the long, narrow garden and over the two terraces before the house, and by the roof a linking of life inside and outside was to be made possible. Simultaneously with the revision of the house and its completion with the transparent living area, a swimming pond was also planned. Originally a spectacular swimming pool, springing out twelve meters into the garden area, which sloped up sharply to the rear, was supposed to complete the modern architecture of the house. But in the end it was to be different.

For various reasons, the idea of the bold swimming pool could not be realized. Through his personal acquaintance with a professional swimming-pond builder, the businessman got the idea of putting in a natural pond for swimming instead of the architecturally bold pool project. Doubts at first—"I had feared that a swimming pond could not work on this strongly sloping ground"—were disposed of in the planning stage by the experienced swimming-pond builders. On a high area in the back part of the garden, a suitable spot for the body of water was found. Because the approach to the garden wound no longer have been possible after the revision of the house, both projects—house and garden pond—were taken up simultaneously. The pond was finished after only four weeks, but the addition to the house extended over a year and a half. So the owner and his family had the possibility of enjoying their first swimming fun while the workers were busy with the house. Equipped with towels and sunshades, they passed by the building site to their newly built swimming pond in the quiet back part of the garden.

Variety is Trump

The swimming pond, up to two meters deep has a sandy shore on which the grandchildren can safely explore nature. Part of the swimming area is only 1.40 meters deep and laid out with stones. It invites a group to play waterball there. The stones on the bottom prevent slipping on the smooth foil. The brave even dare a bold plunge from a diving stone into the refreshing water. The regeneration area is separated by a wall extending to just under the water level, so that the substrata in the plant zone are not stirred up by the swimmers. A walkway that runs around three sides, made of weather-resistant larch wood and extended by a broad wooden deck on the shore, invites all kinds of spare-time activities and allows one to "travel with the sun" during the day. Garden lights make sure that the layout can also unfold its whole splendor in the evening. Since the layout

Steps and decks of larch wood enclose this swimming pond on three sides. On the open side the clearing zone adjoins, its transition to the solid ground defined by a gravel area.

was based completely on individual desires, not only the swimming pond but also the terrain around it, once an isolated corner, have become a frequently visited and used part of the garden.

Attractive All Year

Old trees and the view of the surrounding green hills form a suitable frame for this splendid piece of managed nature. The trees are far enough from the pond so that falling autumn leaves are scarcely a problem. Because the distance to the house is quite long, a bath-house with a small kitchen, refrigerator and coffee machine was built right near the pond. Thus the family can spend long summer days pleasantly and casually in their very private spare-time layout with its swimming pond, which replaces many a short vacation. Since the swimming pond has been finished, the owner and his wife have breakfast as often as possible on the shore of the nearly natural body of bathing water. "The swimming pond has become a second center

in our dwelling life," he acknowledges. And that does not just apply to the summer months: In winter too, they like to gather by the frozen pond, make a few circles on skates, and warm their cold fingers on roasted chestnuts.

Data and Facts

Year Built:
2002

Water Surface:
Swimming area: 24 square meters
Regeneration Area: 28 square meters
Total: 52 square meters

Water Depth:
1.40 to 2.0 meters

Swimming and Regeneration Area Border:
Angular elements

Technical Equipment:
1 biotope carbonator
1 pump
1 skimmer

Formative Elements:
Dry wall
Diving stone
Deck

Planning and Building:
Biotop Landschaftsgestaltung GmbH
A-3411 Weidling

Irregularly laid stepping stones lead to the pond and lead the way to adventure.

Right: *A layout that shows that even a rugged piece of land has room for swimming.*

Ecological Awareness for House and Pond

The Passive House is Ideally Completed by a Swimming pond

This swimming pond with a total area of 100 square meters was built in 2003 even before the house was finished. Since the pond was already finished in April, the owners could use it fully during the building phase. They moved into the modern passive house in August of the same year. The practical form of the house facade is reflected in the geometrically shaped pond, which borders directly on the terrace and is used intensively by the owners during the season.

Why it was to be a Swimming Pond

From the start, the owners had a swimming pond in mind along with the building of the new house. A conventional pool was never considered, on account of the chemical preparation of the water. The owners decided on a biologically cleared swimming pond when the lady of the house, during her further education in the field of garden and landscape work in 2001, came in contact with the concept of a swimming pond. A garden-building firm that specialized in swimming ponds provided planning that convinced her at once. Because a technologically supported swimming pond needs less effort than a purely biologically functioning biotope, the owners decided in favor of this variation.

Maintenance

The installation of technology in the form of pumps, skimmers and carbonators, though, means more work in terms of maintenance. At the end of the swimming season, the entire technology is winterized and stored frost-free until the season begins at the end of March.

Otherwise the usual care is given to this swimming pond, so that the plants in and by the water do not take the upper hand. Trimming off wilted plants in winter takes just an hour's time. Cleaning the pond bottom and removing mud and sediment in the spring are bigger jobs, requiring several hours, depending on the amount of dirt. During the season, algae must be fished out with a net now and then, and the vegetation in some areas must be cut back. The preparations for the winter include cleaning the pond bottom again, which takes another three to four hours of work.

A gravel-strewn area formed of grasses and boulders along the shore creates a harmonious transition to the dry land.

Left: *The clear form of the modern house is reflected in this swimming pond bordering directly on the terrace.*

Life in the Pond

Because the owners know that a swimming pond is not a sterile pool, the pond bottom [p. 68] is not cleaned constantly during the swimming season. That is good for the creatures that live in the pond. Besides beetles, dragonfly larvae and salamanders, frogs also hop around the pond in tadpole time. From the terrace and the wooden deck that projects into the water surface, many of the pond dwellers can be observed easily. The flying skill of the dragonflies in particular is always fascinating. Despite the closeness of the swimming pond to the house, there are no problems with mosquitoes, which the owners attribute to the animal life in the water.

Children Love Ponds

Many pond owners worry when small children go near the water. The owners of this swimming pond also have a small child who likes to bathe in the soft, biologically cleared water. Their five-month-old daughter Lara first took a baby swimming course at the local swimming pool to learn to deal with water and encounter the cool liquid without fear. Supported by a swimming board, the girl, now two years old, now makes her circles in the family's own swimming pond. To rule out any risk, though, the parents advise all pond owners never to let small children or those who cannot swim play alone in the water.

A sunshade provides shade for the sitting place that projects into the swimming pond.

Data and Facts

Year Built:
2003

Water Surface:
Swimming area: 50 square meters
Regeneration area: 50 square meters
Total: 100 square meters

Water Depth:
2.0 meters

Swimming and Regeneration Area Border:
Concrete wall

Technical equipment:
Water circulation
1 biotope carbonator
1 skimmer

Formative Elements:
Wooden decks and sitting place by the pond
Field of fine gravel

Planning and Building:
Biotop Landschaftsgestaltung GmbH
A-3411 Weidling

Dream House by Dream Pond

The owner of this swimming pond, in his capacity as an independent building contractor, had already built several conventional swimming pools before he thought about planning a body of bathing water for himself. A swimming pond, as big as possible, was to border directly on the terrace, in order to make the water as accessible as possible. Since the builder had already converted an old existing swimming pool into a swimming biotope at a customer's wish, he knew that a swimming pond fits better into the landscape of a garden than a conventional pool does. The decision to plan his own

From the edge of the left side of the terrace, an easy step on the wooden stairs gives easy access to the pond. On the opposite shore, an arched bridge spans the swimming pond. It separates a spring hill with a fountain from the actual pond.

pond as a biotope was thus almost self-evident for the nature-oriented builder: "Every person has different needs; one likes extremely clear water, but I prefer it natural. Thus I worked with biotopes and knew that was absolutely what I wanted to build."

A Private Spare Time Center

Because of the size of the pond and the planned depth of some four meters, the building work included much excavation of soil that had to be taken away. Neighbors and passers-by thought that, what with the busy activity and large pit, a spare-time center was to be built there. When only one family used the layout after it had been finished, the regret for the public success of the spare-time park was probably a reason for some people to sneer. But the owners enjoy the exclusive quality of the large swimming pond all the more.

Biotope Carbonator Against Algae

The finished pond adjoins the terrace in a kidney-shaped curve. An artificial brook course, a spring hill with a fountain, and a wide regeneration area adjoining the pond on three sides link the pond to the surrounding garden landscape. Two wooden decks and an arched bridge allow close observation of the plants and animals in the regeneration zone. With an over-average depth of up to four meters, the water in the swimming zone stays pleasantly fresh even in summer heat. Two skimmers collect coarse particles from the water surface, and in the evening the layout can be illuminated by several underwater spotlights. For water clearing, the repositioning plants in the clearing zone are supported by a biotope carbonator. The installation of the carbonator was done later, as it was seen in the first summer that the situation of the pond, facing directly southward, and the sun rays reflected by the white walls of the house made the pH value of the water rise and thus influenced algae growth excessively but inhibited the growth of the oxygen-forming underwater plants. After the carbonator was installed, the algae problem was solved and no further difficulties appeared.

Maintenance

The care of the unusually large and deep swimming pond requires somewhat more time and skill than a typical layout. During the swimming season, the skimmers are emptied regularly. In winter the plants are cut back to the height of the water surface, which takes about five hours' time. In spring a so-called "small pond service" comes due, takes half a day and is carried out by a local firm that specializes in building swimming ponds. Because of the unusual depth of four meters, cleaning the pond bottom is a bit more laborious than otherwise but can still be handled. Then the water is so clear that one can see to the bottom. The owner always cuts the plants back when it is necessary. He uses ordinary garden shears and, for the underwater plants, a special underwater scythe.

Greatest Possible Depth

The convinced swimming-pond owner advises all who are interested in a natural body of swimming water to make the pond as deep as possible. Cleaning it is somewhat more expensive than for shallow ponds, but the good water quality rewards the extra effort. In general, he urges them to remember that one should follow a certain way of building a pond not only because it is trendy, which can sometimes lead to great disappointment. He himself has never regretted his decision in favor of a swimming pond and particularly enjoys lying on an air mattress in the water, closing his eyes and listening to the splashing of the spring. And although he had expected that more mosquitoes could appear in the still water right by the house, experience has taught him better. Probably the frogs, toads, dragonflies and other animals living in the pond contribute to natural pest control. Early in the summer the croaking of frogs briefly becomes so loud that one can scarcely converse on the terrace, but the nature-loving owners do not let themselves be disturbed by it, for by August at the latest, a quiet paradise prevails again in the very private spare-time park.

Data and Facts

Year Built:
1995

Water Surface:
Swimming area: 115 square meters
Regeneration zone: 135 square meters
Total: 250 square meters

Water Depth:
4.0 meters

Technical Equipment:
2 water circulators
2 skimmers
2 biotope carbonators
3 underwater spotlights in swimming area
5 underwater spotlights in regeneration area

Formative Elements:
2 platforms
1 bridge (span 6 meters)
Artificial stream course
Spring hill with fountain

Planning and Building:
Biotop Landschaftsgestaltung GmbH
A-3411 Weidling

Right: *This large swimming pond wraps itself in organic form around the wide, extensive terrace on the garden side of the house.*

Swimming Landscape for Guests

The owner of a hotel in the vacation paradise of Meran, South Tyrol, planned while rebuilding and renovating the hotel to make the existing swimming pool from the 1960s more attractive and integrate it better into the formal garden that was formed with much love and knowledge of the subject. On the ground floor of the hotel a new indoor swimming pool had already been built. From there the guests should be able to go through the sunbathing meadow to the outdoor pool, which would enrich the amenities more in the warm months. The hotel-owning family, always close to nature and gardens, had learned from trade papers that it is possible to lay out a swimming pond without chemical water preparation. This suited the hotel concept, corresponded with the owner's wishes for a natural pond, and would also have the advantage of making the hotel different from others.

Natural water or swimming pond: The pond blends perfectly with the surrounding landscape.

Official Permission for Rebuilding

In planning the rebuilding in 2004, a firm that specialized in building swimming ponds was called in from Austria, as the local firms did not have sufficient experience in building public swimming ponds. Along with the steep slope of the property, the requirements of the Italian authorities at first made the project problematic. The swimming pond could have a maximum depth of only 1.4 meters; otherwise a lifeguard would have to be employed for its use to be allowed. Concrete could not be used for construction because of landscape protection. Under these limitations, the angled-element building style was chosen, and was recognized by the Italian authorities as conforming to the landscape. A large regeneration area and an additional plant filter provide maximum water quality. Wooden platforms on the shore invite guests to stay and allow examination of the vegetation. Garden lighting is enhanced with underwater lighting, allowing the swimming pond to be used during the evenings.

Original Concerns Disposed

After the opening of the renovated and re-built hotel in April 2004, there was concern at first as to whether the south-west situation of the pond and the modest water depth would lead to complications in water clearing in the Mediterranean climate of Meran on account of too-strong sunlight and heat. After the first swimming season, though, the concerns were ruled out. The owners report happily that there are no water quality problems.

Care of the Swimming Water

The amount of care in which the pond owner is supported by the pond-building firm is modest for the still very new swimming pond, the owner reports. The skimmers are cleaned once a day, the filters in the machine room once a week. Every two months a mud-sucking

Evening atmosphere with a view over the swimming pond and into the valley.
Underwater lighting allows use of the swimming area even at nightfall.

device is used in the pond so that no slippery layer of sediment builds up. When the plants in the regeneration have settled, they will need to be cut back at times.

Fulfilled Dreams

In other ways too, the expectations of the owners were completely fulfilled: The new swimming pond blends splendidly into the garden, better than any conventional swimming pool. "The swimming pond is our pride and joy," the owner's daughter affirms. The initial skepticism that the green-colored water and the pond foil, which was somewhat slippery at the start, could be seen negatively by the guests gave way to passionate enthusiasm. The feminine hotel guests in particular are impressed by the water quality, since it—unlike chemically treated water—does not dry out the skin at all. Whoever still swears by bathing in turquoise-blue water always has the alternative of using the indoor pool. But if one looks over the garden and at the valley and the breathtaking Alpine panorama,

the choice of where one will enjoy the nicer swimming pleasure should not be difficult.

The swimming pond can be used by all hotel guests and enjoys great popularity.

Data and Facts

Year Built:
2005

Water Surface:
Swimming area: 81 square meters
Regeneration area: 92 square meters, including
Plant filter: 46 square meters
Total: 173 square meters

Water Depth:
1.4 meters

Technical Equipment:
Water circulation
1 pump
2 skimmers
Underwater spotlights

Formative Elements:
Wooden platforms and decks on the shore
Sunbathing area

Planning and Building:
Biotop Landschaftsgestaltung GmbH
A-3411 Weidling

Swimming Pleasure with Lake View

Curving shapes, wise formative principles and natural materials characterize this swimming-pond project, which was realized on a slope overlooking Lake Zuerich. The owner, a specialist in the realms of nutrition, esoterics and feng-shui, and her husband always lived on Lake Zuerich and always had a close relationship to the water. Several years ago, when they turned their house on the lake over to their son and moved into a 300-year-old house overlooking the lake and protected as a monument, they missed the closeness to the water for the first time. So they decided to bring the water to their door.

A Biotope in a Landscape Protection Area

"A swimming pool would never have been considered. First because we are very aware of ecology and take good care of the environment," the owner relates, "and second because our property is in a landscape protection area where no new structures may be built." The project was almost wiped out by landscape protection, for the Swiss authorities at first refused to allow a swimming pond to be built. "On the second try we succeeded, because we were able to blend the biotope (which our swimming pond is now called officially) lovingly into the landscape." A brook course, large stairs from the house down to the pond, and a sitting place above the swimming pond with a splendid view of Lake Zuerich show that they succeeded.

"Sitting Stairs" by the Pond

To build the pond, the sharply sloping meadow in front of the house had to be terraced. This created several "activity zones" which—unlike the former steep slope—could now be used intensively. Broad sandstone steps, broken by lawn areas, lead down to the pond. The owner praises the advantages of this layout. "For us

they are sitting steps. According to our moods, we sit on the rim and read a book. Or we go two steps farther down and wallow in the water. A little farther and we find ourselves in another 'climate zone'. Because of the steps, swimming has become almost secondary for us."

Care is "Light"

Garden work is not work; everyone who has eagerly taken up this green hobby knows that. The owner of this swimming pond does not go to the garden with a stopwatch, even though she also tends an ecologically oriented vegetable garden. How much time she applies to pond care she can thus not say precisely. Once a year, in the spring, she has a firm come in to handle the crudest cleaning jobs in the pond. Otherwise] she lets the pond take care of itself most of the time. Only now and then does she cut some plants back. "I clean the natural stone

Harmoniously settled in the landscape, this pond forms an inviting swimming terrace.

steps to the water regularly, though, because that is the place where we like to spend a lot of time."

Creativity Pays

With so much enthusiasm, it is evident that the decision in favor of the swimming pond was never regretted. The owner advises builders with similar steeply sloping property not to shy away from terracing the slope, despite the added expense. The terraces multiply the useful surface of the garden. She sees the confident cooperation with a competent specialist firm, which also resulted in creative negotiations with the authorities, as great luck. And she has another tip for future swimming-pond builders: One should have tolerance for nature. "When I found a lot of algae damage in the pond in

the first months, I said to myself, the pond has to find itself. One can and should not want to determine everything. Man must have the greatness to let things run. Whoever has this attitude will be just as lucky with his swimming pond as I am."

Data and Facts

Year Built:
2005

Water Surface:
Swimming area: 58 square meters
Regeneration area: 64 square meters
Plant filter: 10 square meters
Total: 132 square meters

Water Depth:
2.0 meters

Technical Equipment:
Water circulation
Pump
Skimmer
Biotope carbonator with injector jet
Plant filter

Formative Elements:
Dry wall of sandstone blocks
Wide sitting stairs of sandstone blocks by the water

Planning and Building:
Egli Gartenbau AG
CH-8646 Wagen SG

The steps lead directly to the water, creating a romantic atmosphere ...

__Right__: The variety of this layout makes the swimming pond an experience.

Swimming Pond with Nordic Character

This swimming pond, given a prize by a specialist jury, blends into the environment especially harmoniously with its curved shores. The rounded shapes are continued in the formation of the large platform, at the end of which wooden stairs lead to the entrance to the swimming area. The swimming pond of some 120 square meters is defined by a wall and has two clearing areas with plants. A brook flows into one of the regeneration zones and, with its soft splashing, helps create a relaxed atmosphere for swimming as well as the bordering, imaginatively paved terrace. The dry wall of naturally rounded granite boulders, piled on each other in the style of a frieze wall, and the green-planted wooden roof of the bathing cabin provide a breath of robust Scandinavian originality. Yet the layout is planned to the last detail and equipped with the newest technology: a biotope carbonator, an animal-friendly surface skimmer, and a pump for the brook. Through good planning and practical pond technology, the clarity of the water, 1.90 meters deep, is splendid.

The green-planted bathing cabin snuggles into the slope and creates a pleasant archaic atmosphere.

Data and Facts

Year Built:
2003

Water Surface:
Swimming area: 60 square meters
Regeneration zone: 35 square meters
Plant filter: 25 square meters
Total: 120 square meters

Water Depth:
1.90 meters

Technical Equipment:
Pump
Skimmer
Biotope carbonator
Plant filter

Formative Elements:
Curving platform and separate sun deck
Dry wall of granite pieces
Bathing cabin with green-planted roof

Planning and Building:
Bahl Garten, Landschafts &
Schwimmteichbau
D-25368 Kiebitzreihe

An elegantly curving wooden platform connects the area around the bathing cabin with the back garden and another wooden deck.

Swimming Pond Instead of Vacation

The owner of this swimming pond wanted to devote his vacation, as usual, to relaxation and recreation. But because he is the manager of a garden-building firm, which also builds swimming ponds, he was so enthusiastic about the principle of natural swimming waters that he gave up his vacation and laid out a private swimming pond in his own garden in the hot summer of 2003. Although he gave up his whole vacation, his family is enthusiastic now as then: "The longer we have had the pond, the happier we are about the decision that was not easy then, but was right, and that fills us with pride." Meanwhile the pond is inspired at least once a day to experience all kinds of changes. Every spring it fascinates the family anew to see the tadpoles grow up to be frogs and watch the dragonfly larvae grow into "land-based" flying acrobats. At first a curious gray heron visited the new body of water. But since there were no fish in the pond and thus no food for the bird, he soon lost interest. But it was very different for the family's two daughters: They learned to swim in their own pond.

Aqua-Jogging in the Swimming Pond

Good things take time. That is also true of building swimming ponds. From the first idea to the completion of the project, a good two years passed. The present swimming-pond owners first came in contact with friends with biologically cleared swimming water. When invited, they swam in the swimming pond and were totally enthused from then on, and convinced that they too had to have such a swimming pond. Shortly thereafter they made contact with the firm that had built their friends' pond. After the first consultation, a drawing was made and an offer tendered. After that came a year of thinking. Finally there was another conference, and a planning contract for a biologically cleared swimming pond, complete with surroundings, was signed.

Variety in Small Space

The outdoor area has three different sitting places, each allowing a different view of the pond and being in the sun at a different time of the day. The swimming pond, built around a corner of the house, with a wide wooden platform also intended as a sun deck, offers a different view from each perspective. With an area of 40 square meters in all, this swimming pond is not one of the big ones, but it is useful in various ways thanks to competent planning. A shallow wading area for children, with a gravel bottom, is used intensively by the family's two sons, eleven and seven years old.

Advantage: Outside Shower

Through cleverly installed lighting in and by the pond, the garden and water invite one for relaxing hours in the evening and on warm summer nights. A stainless steel shower installed in the surrounding area near the pond is an added attraction. The model was designed by an acquaintance especially for the owners, and inspired the pond-building firm to offer outdoor showers with future projects.

A Pond for Everyone

Meanwhile, the pond has become a central point in the family's life. From a water temperature of 18 degrees C up, they swim practically every day. Right after they come home from school, the boys jump into the cool water, and the man of the house, who has a business, spends practically all of his lunch break at the pool. The lady of the house uses the pond for aqua-jogging and other sports activities. For this family, a life without a swimming pond is no longer imaginable.

Data and Facts

Year Built:
2004

Water Surface:
Swimming area: 20 square meters
Regeneration area: 13 square meters
Plant filter: 7 square meters
Total: 40 square meters

Water Depth:
2.0 meters

Technical Equipment:
None

Formative Elements:
Curving wooden platform
Fountain stone
Shallow water area for children

Planning and Building:
Helmut Haas GmbH & Co.
D-88239 Wangen-Roggenzell

A successful example of a small but versatile and interestingly formed pool.

Country Garden with Swimming Pond

Chlorine-free and yet pure—that was the dream of the owners for their own swimming water ever since their student days. An old rest home on the lower Rhine finally offered the chance to realize their long-held wish. On the property, which measured more than 3000 square meters in all, behind the rest home's old garage, a beautiful water landscape arose, with the help of a garden architect and a contractor who specialized in building swimming ponds, a paradise surrounded by numerous sitting places and opened by meandering sand paths covered with crushed dolomite sand. The swimming pond, with a swimming zone of more than a hundred square meters, has curving contours instead of square corners, thus blending harmoniously into the rural garden landscape.

From Orchard to Swimming Paradise

The ground was an old orchard before it was restructured. For years, superfluous building material had been stored there, nettles and wild alders, willows and birches had grown up, and the old fruit trees had survived without regular care. Thus many of the old trees had to be removed; only one old cherry tree and a few other fruit trees could be saved. To divide up the plot of land, several hedges were planted. Along with one free-growing hedge that offers privacy along the boundary, various shaped hedges separate individual sections of the garden, so that a manifold garden landscape has been created. In all, five sitting places were set up in the garden and always invite one to pleasant togetherness or relaxed observation of the flora and fauna by the pond. A path around the pond leads to ever-new, surprising perspectives in the various garden areas.

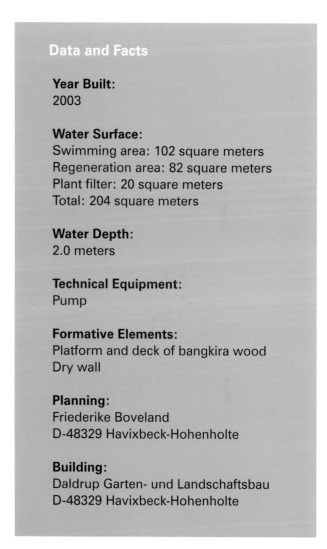

Data and Facts

Year Built:
2003

Water Surface:
Swimming area: 102 square meters
Regeneration area: 82 square meters
Plant filter: 20 square meters
Total: 204 square meters

Water Depth:
2.0 meters

Technical Equipment:
Pump

Formative Elements:
Platform and deck of bangkira wood
Dry wall

Planning:
Friederike Boveland
D-48329 Havixbeck-Hohenholte

Building:
Daldrup Garten- und Landschaftsbau
D-48329 Havixbeck-Hohenholte

Left and right: *A pond ideally set in its surroundings. Here one can let his mind roll on and enjoy relaxed hours.*

Water as a Very Special Garden Experience

Like the central point of the whole garden, the swimming pond, already built several years ago and nicely grown in since then, lies in its park-like surroundings, a large garden. The varying planting of the grounds with flowerbeds and decorative trees and bounded by older trees, combines with the large mowed lawns to form a suitable frame for the natural swimming pond. A wellness house with sauna and resting room expands the uses of the grounds and increases their spare-time value. The owners of this swimming pond became aware of the concept of biologically cleared swimming ponds from newspaper articles. In addition, an acquaintance had already had a swimming pond built, so that they could gain a direct impression of the advantages of such an ecologically valuable swimming basin. At a garden fair the now proud owner of the pond met the manager of a garden-building firm that also builds swimming ponds. But at first there was a problem: Where should the pond be placed? With the desired dimensions, the project could not be placed in the existing garden without changes. Only after the neighboring plot of land was put up for sale and could be bought was it possible to make the dream come true.

Convincing Reasons

Before the final decision, numerous talks were had with the specialist of the garden-building firm. They also visited several already-built swimming ponds before the building finally began. Thus the arguments for and against a swimming pond with biological water clearing could be weighed carefully and all questions answered in advance. The preparations paid for themselves, as the owners declare today: "We did not want to do without the swimming pond any longer. Water in the garden always develops into the focal point, and when it can also be swum in, the garden experience is all the nicer." The thoroughly positive reactions from friends and acquaintances gave further assurance that the decision for the swimming pond was right. The satisfied owner advises all future swimming-pond builders; "Do not build the swimming pond too small at all. One must be able to swim a few strokes. If there is not enough space, one is better off raising koi carp in the pond."

Data and Facts

Year Built:
2001

Water Surface:
Swimming area: 80 square meters
Regeneration area: 40 square meters
Plant filter: 40 square meters
Total: 160 square meters

Water Depth:
2.0 meters

Technical Equipment:
Water circulation
Pump
2 skimmers
Biotope-carbonator with injector jet
Plant filter
3 fountain stones

Formative Elements:
Wooden platform and large wooden deck
Garden with park character and much planting
Wellness house with sauna and resting room by the pond

Planning and Building:
Bahl Garten-, Landschafts- und Schwimmteichbau
D-25368 Kiebitzreihe

The big swimming area is even enough for families with sporting ambitions.
The necessary space was available after the neighboring lot was bought.

The winter garden joins living and spare-time areas. From here one can enjoy a look at the water, even on cold days.

The path between the house and pond was created with much love and detail. A shaped boxwood hedge borders the path.

Swimming Ponds in Hanging Gardens

Before the building of this large swimming pond in a garden measuring some 500 square meters could begin, the sloping land first had to be terraced. With walls of light gray rectangular granite blocks, the garden was divided into several large steps of varying sizes. The swimming pond takes up the entire lowest level, and thus almost half of the whole plot. The special feature of this biologically cleared body of bathing water is the swimming basin, which was covered in polished stainless steel instead of pond foil. The clear contours of the basin and the atmospherically shimmering water that reflects the sunbeams speak for this unusual solution.

Granite as the Theme

The shoreline areas, of varying width and planted with repositioning plants, are bordered with light gray granite pieces. Granite blocks support the steep slope. The steps are made of the same stone, as is the small paved area beside the pond, which borders on the boundary line. Spheres cut out of granite were placed beside the pond as fountain stones and comfort the senses with their soft splashing, no matter whether one betakes himself into the pond or relaxes on the wooden deck beside the pond.

Spheres and Columns

A well-thought planting with Japanese maple *(Acer palmatum* 'Fireglow'), columnar and spherical trees like shaped boxwood *(Buxus)*, Serbian firs *(Picea omorica),* columnar European hornbeam *(Carpinus betulus 'Fastigiata')* and evergreen hedge plants like laurel cherry *(Prunus lauocerasus)* and yew *Taxus baccata)* frame the swimming pond on three sides and give privacy from curious looks from the neighborhood. Between the living area and the swimming pond, the sitting place built of teak creates an ideal link invites one to take the sun and relax, not only in swimming pauses.

From here on, a footbridge crosses the narrow regeneration zone and allows easy access to the swimming pond on a stainless steel ladder.

Data and Facts

Year Built:
2004

Water Surface:
Swimming area: 70 square meters
Regeneration area: 70 square meters
Total: 140 square meters

Water Depth:
2,0 meters

Technical Equipment:
Swimming area separation with stainless steel wall modules
Completely protected pond watertightness with natural stone
(gravel, natural stone slabs)
3 circulation pumps, skimmer, fountain element
Automatic water-level regulation
3 underwater sprays
Pump shaft with automatic time-setting

Formative Elements:
Basin covering of stainless steel
Deck of teak
Wall of quartzite blocks
Platform of teak
Granite spheres as fountain stones

Planning and Building:
Garten- und Landschaftsbau Pohl GmbH
D-93497 Willmering

Left: *The spherical fountain stone is an eye-catcher by the naturally planted edge of the swimming pond.*

Pond Landscapes for Romantics

What we consider beautiful, and whether we do, depends strongly on the proportions. And it is the right proportions that have contributed to the success of this romantic pond landscape. House, water and garden have been combined to make a harmonious whole. Viewing directions follow the lines of the house and create a link between architecture and nature. Thus the rectangular granite fountain-stone slabs lengthen the central axis of the house and lead the eyes from the dining room over the pond to the opposite shore. There is a special charm in the contrast between the "hard" and "soft" shore areas, the terrace of the house and the natural pond shore with its thick planting.

Garden Pavilion for Dreamy Hours

A narrow path paved with cinder blocks connects the circular filigreed pavilion directly to the house terrace. The pavilion itself was adorned with grapevines, and the surroundings are also luxuriantly planted. Thus the impression of a lake pavilion amid a park landscape is created. This impression is strengthened by

Left and right: *Viewing axes and a balanced formation give the impression of an English landscape park.*

making the path to the house not straight, but angled. Thus this idyllic garden pavilion, lighted at night, has become the whole family's favorite place, space to celebrate with friends, play, sunbathe and relax. From here, the view extends over a big water axis some thirty meters long, on the end of which a wide, round sitting place covered with gravel is located.

Formative Ideas Around the Pond

Pond landscapes, no matter whether they are of natural origin or were created by man according to his conceptions and needs, are above all oases of rest and places to relax and recover. For children and young people, the pond in their own garden also means fun and pleasure, by which adults are inspired all too gladly. Whoever is open to changes and gives his imagination free rein can create from a wealth of formative ideas and thus spend his days around the swimming pond with more variety and intenseness.

One With Nature

Conventional swimming pools are found, unfortunately all too often, isolated from the rest of the garden, in a monotonous lawn or concrete terrace. Swimming ponds made after nature's model, on the other hand, can be made by careful planning and formation and good care into a harmonious part of the surroundings and become one with nature. In an ideal case they combine the idyllic beauty of a quiet lake with the practical advantages of a many-sided spare-time layout right by the house.

Primary activities are naturally those like bathing, swimming and wading, the main reasons for building a swimming pond. Thanks to a nicely formed environment, sunbathing, observing life by and in the pond, celebrating with friends or simply enjoying an hour of relaxing and doing nothing rank among the privileges that one can enjoy as a swimming-pond owner—and almost any time, for one's own spare-time park is open nonstop, day and night, in any season! And something else makes the

decision for a swimming pond easy: Whether spring, summer, autumn or winter—a pond is always a visible enrichment for the garden. This is true not only in the summer months in which the swimming pond is used often for swimming. The real value of the body of water that is made to resemble nature is revealed particularly in the cold winter months, when the water is drained from conventional swimming pools. The swimming pond, on the other hand, is at attraction in the garden all winter. Shore plants can be just as charming in late autumn as grass sparkling with frost.

The Pond by the House

In the most recent years, the sun deck by the pond has been combined more and more often with the terrace of the house, not least because the costs of the house and swimming pond can be reduced considerably when built at the same time. The closeness of the pond to the terrace also invites spontaneous, refreshing bathing and moves it into the center of events. In an extensive garden, owners often deliberately place their swimming pond away from the house. Setting it in the garden landscape increases the value of the experience when bathing and the path to the pond makes bathing a conscious spare-time pleasure. The distance from the house and the available space also offer the possibility of adding formative elements like bath-houses, showers or sculptures. It should be kept in mind when planning that the rest of the garden should not be cut off from the house by the swimming pond.

Right: *Platforms join the water landscape.*

Left: *The swimming pond emphasizes the rural charm of the rustic scene.*

Space to Play and Splash

A swimming pond framed by luxuriant vegetation, on which water lilies bloom, where cattails and purple loosestrife wave in the wind and dragonflies make their rounds over the water, looks venerable and wild and awakens the interest in knowing the water landscape and all its secrets better. Visitors need not push their way through the shore vegetation first, for the pond is reachable all around with paths or naturally formed shore zones. Platforms and stepping stones that extend into the pond invite a nearer approach to the water. Thus one can have a look at the animal and plant world in the shallow water without getting wet feet.

And what pond owner has not discovered that he spends more time on the shore than he had planned because, for example, a bright, shimmering dragonfly emerges from its unlikely chitinous armor and he does not want to miss this natural drama. Others spend hours in the middle of the regeneration zone, sitting on stepping stones or boulders, thinking, observing or reading a book. Everyone finds his favorite place and creates recreation and rest from the time he spends by the pond.

Flat Gravel: Beach for Children

For children in particular, splashing and unrestrained playing are great pleasures. Thus when planning, be sure to include a special place for the "young folks."

Children's bathing areas that are structurally separated from the adults' swimming areas are becoming more and more popular. The water in this zone can be changed easily and also warms up more quickly in summer than in the swimming area. But children do not always share in this rational solution, and all too often they want to join the "big folks" in the deep basin. To create a spatial separation and thus relax the children's isolation, shore areas after the model of natural swimming lakes, that slope gradually to the swimming area, can be planned. There the whole family can bathe together safely.

The realization of this idea, of course, requires more space for the swimming pond, since the gravel beach must be kept flat to avoid slipping. The tilt of the bottom in the water should have a ratio of one in ten. Thus there is a space of some eight to ten meters needed from the shoreline to the end of the flat area. If the garden does not have this much space, then the swimming area for the adults may need to be reduced. Pond owners who are both devoted parents and enthusiastic swimmers will understand.

A Sandy Beach in the Garden

Scarcely any other shore formation inspires such a vacation mood as a sandy beach on the swimming pond. At the same time, it is the ideal completion for the flat beach. The open, happy atmosphere that comes from the fine sandy beach is incomparable. Here children find a place for untroubled playing, and adults can let their spirits rise too.

Are Sandy Beaches Possible Everywhere?

Laying a sandy beach by a swimming pond is especially simple in regions where the soil naturally has a high sand content. In Germany, sandy soil is found, for example, in Hamburg, in Berlin and the Markish land around it, and in the coastal regions on the North and Baltic Seas. There, after building a swimming pond, one need only spread a wheelbarrow of washed river sand on the flat shore and spread it around. But a capillary block has to be planned for the shore of the swimming pond, so the water table has no contact with the beach.

The transition zone from the sandy beach to the water must be made with a special lot of care. Sand carried into the water gradually sinks to the deepest part of the swimming area and must then be removed from the bottom of the pond. To reduce the movement to a minimum, it is a good idea to add a gravel covering to about a meter and a half above the shoreline. This catches sand washed down by rain and also reduces the sand brought there by bathers. Here too it is recommended that a capillary block—the shoreline bar—be placed as near the sandy beach as possible and then buried under the gravel.

Spreading the Sand

If no naturally sandy soil is at hand, laying a real "beach" is clearly more difficult. Before spreading the sand, the whole soil near the shore should be dug out to a depth of up to 30 centimeters. Though one would just as soon spread the sand on the soil by the shore, the rain would wash it away in a short time. A high addition of gravel doers not help, nor does the shoreline bar. If the sandy beach is laid as horizontally as possible, this will also hinder the sand from caving in and washing away.

To prevent the growth of unwanted vegetation, a special water-permeable foil from the garden shop can be laid.

Whether public or private—a sandy beach by a swimming pond means a vacation from everyday life.

A Field for Sunbathing

If the swimming pond does not directly adjoin the terrace or a sitting place, one needs a halfway dry, even place near the sun deck to dry out, rest or sunbathe. On slopes in particular, paved sitting places can be built only with a lot of trouble. The simplest thing here, as also on flat land, is to put in a lawn that invites one to stretch out and sunbathe after swimming, and becomes a play meadow for children. So that grass grows well, one needs a high-quality seed mixture, a sunny location and a not too stony soil. Often the ground around a swimming pond was much compacted by building machines and excavators during construction. In such cases a deep loosening of the soil is recommended before seeding, so that later no puddles occur.

A Shower by the Swimming Pond

Showering before jumping into the water, customary if not required at public pools, is becoming more and more popular in the private sector too, although the water in a private pond is scarcely polluted by the users without showering. For one's own garden, original solutions are available, ranging from designer showers to solar types. The latter have the advantage of letting one shower warm—and that without having to provide a connection to the electric or hot water system near the location.

With a one-hand mixer one can regulate the water temperature without losing water. This is especially advantageous in solar showers, where only a limited amount of warm water is available.

The floor of the shower can be made of the same boards as the sun deck. A deep bet of gravel underneath prevents flooding the surrounding area.

Lawns and wooden decks near the swimming pond invite sunbathing.

Showers by the swimming pond should be functional and simple to use.

96

Brooks and Waterfalls

A very popular and often-used formative element in a garden is a stream bed. Pond fans want most of all to hear the splashing of water. Moving water suggests freshness, though there is self-deception involved. In simple stream courses, the water is simply pumped up to the spring and then flows down and back to the pond without any freshening or cleaning. Contrary to popular opinion, the water in an artificial brook is not enriched with oxygen, not even at night. In the daytime, when the brook is in action, even the oxygen produced by the algae is driven out and the concentration is reduced. Yet a brook fitted to the terrain is always a visual enrichment.

Land that slopes down eases the natural construction of a stream bed and also allows the building of a water-collecting basin at the top of the course. Like a swimming pond, a brook course is also laid out with pond foil, and the edges of the foil are covered with gravel. On flat land the terrain has to be modified appropriately to create a slight slope.

Artificial Stream Courses

Sometimes the soil dug out of a swimming pond site is piled up near the shore so as to let a brook flow from there into the pond. In such a solution, the pile of soil can be an artificial effective element. If the stream course then leads downhill in several S-bends, the impression that it makes can scarcely be surpassed. Such a scene contradicts the simple fact that water in nature always finds the shortest way to the valley!

Sometimes small waterfalls are built into the stream bed. More spectacular, though, are waterfalls and cascades that empty dramatically into the swimming pond. Such a spectacle makes bathing more pleasant and attracts children magnetically. The size of a waterfall depends on the pump performance. Pumps that keep the water flow coming use a lot of energy, which has its effect on the electric bill. The running time of pumps can, of course, be controlled by timers, but one should consider that waterless stream beds clearly lack attraction and the shore vegetation by dry waterfalls suffers.

As a charming and unpretentious alternative to a brook, there is the spring stone, which also splashes softly and is also easier to take care of.

Where a natural slope exists, a brook can be the ideal completion to a pond.

Walkways and Bridges

Walkways and bridges are aids to allow walking by and over the water with dry feet. They are usually used with large swimming ponds and public natural bathing beaches. They lead the visitor right to the center of lively action. There they let him experience flora and fauna closely. In private swimming ponds they only make sense when they fulfill a real function. Building one purely for looks is not advised.

Along with their value as observation posts, walkways and bridges can make pond care from the shore easier. Devices such as the underwater scythe have meanwhile become so refined, though, that with the help of telescopic handles they can be used easily from the shore. Where there is no place for a bridge but a connection of the shores is wanted, stepping stones laid on a substructure in the regeneration area can offer a substitute. A good connection of walkways and bridges with the rest of the garden is attained by using gravel, stepping stones set near the bottom, or natural stone paving. Walkways are also the lengthenings and endpoints of paths by and to the water. They allow an easy entrance and exit for the swimming zone only when they are combined with a ladder. Where enough space is available, walkways can expand into sundecks for resting and relaxing.

When are Bridges Practical?

Walkways and arch bridges in private swimming ponds should be built only if one really uses them. For pure decoration they are superfluous and too costly. Their planning requires a lot of fingertip feeling and they can also raise the cost somewhat. Most ponds—often because of limited space in the garden—are not bigger than 100 square meters. Separating this surface by walkways or bridges can take much of its naturalness from the pond and considerably reduce the already limited water surface as well. The pond owner invests a sum of about 250 Euro in every square meter of a pond and makes it

unusable for swimming or regenerating with a walkway that also costs something more. In principle here as in all design decisions, the consideration should be applied as to whether the planned element will really be useful. A bridge that links two shores will never be used if the way around the pond is simpler and safer. Also to be considered is that the mass of a safe arch bridge often does not correspond to the size of a swimming pond—unless the pond is bigger than 200 square meters.

A diving stone on the shore—if firmly anchored, is not just a great spare-time pleasure for children!

Diving Boards

When putting up a diving board, it must be assured that a solid anchoring is guaranteed. The forces that are released by bending a diving board are mighty. The attachment should be on the shore of the pond or on the sun deck along the shore, where a concrete socket can be hidden under the deck boards. Building a diving board usually fails not because of the depth of the swimming pond—1.80 meters will be quite enough—but because of the size and, above all, the length of the swimming area. The radius around the end of the diving board must be at least three meters, so that nobody who dives into the water can be injured on any borders of the swimming area.

When building a diving board, already used materials should be matched. The combination of plastic boards with wooden decks very much detracts from the optical harmony of a pond scene.

Walkways: Home-made, Kits or Finished Products?

When planning a walkway, one should determine what kind of wood one wants to use for the surface, and then stick to his choice. One should never save on the strength of the wood. Thin boards rot quickly and then must be completely replaced. With wood at least four

Bridges are an enrichment only when they form a sensible connection between two shores.

centimeters thick, the cost is higher, nut in the long run one will save a lot of annoyance. Under the effect of the sun, even well-dried wood of the recommended thickness will work well. To avoid warping of the wood, a cleat at least one centimeter thick should be attached in the center of the long dimension (see tips). This cleat reduces the tension in the wood. Also to be avoided are too-long or too-wide walkway boards. A width of some 10 to 15 centimeters and a length of one and a half to two meters, plus a gap of about one centimeter between the boards, are ideal for the job. With these sizes one can use a modular structure (see tips), which allows the boards to be screwed on from below. This not only looks good, but also protects one from injury. In calculating the need for walkway boards, one should also include replacement boards for later repairs.

The piers for wooden walkways and bridges can be made yourself of angled wood. But the trade also offers complete kits. Many firms that specialize in pond equipment have finished walkways and bridges made of wood or other materials (steel or iron, rarely also plastic) in their stocks. Because of the precisely calculated statics of such designs, one is usually well advised to use them, and saves a lot of time. Most manufacturers are also set up to produce special sizes. Bridges that span the pond in a slightly curved arch look especially elegant. Since they are particularly hard to build, it is recommended that unskilled carpenters to use finished products. But whoever wants to do it himself must be sure not to select a too-small radius for the arch bridge, or else uncomfortable climbs can result. A very simple bridge design consists of simple, wide wooden planks that are laid on a concrete abutment of similar stone foundation at both ends. Such a simple walkway looks best when it leads just barely over the water surface. Since walkways can be slippery, especially in spring and autumn, rippled treads are often used. In general, walkways are used with caution, or not used at all, in precipitation storms.

Support Posts for Walkways

Support posts for walkways in swimming or regeneration areas should be set in a foundation of thin concrete. Post shoes of galvanized steel with a finished foundation are a practical alternative. Should a support post in the water not be avoidable, a secure post support is the highest law. Here it is a matter of enlarging the standing surface of the post so that it does not damage the pond foil and will stand securely without wobbling. The simplest method—requiring flat ground—is to use an old auto tire that is filled with concrete and has the post placed in its center. Well-dried "concrete tires" complete with posts can be placed on a thick foil or fleece. There is no less expensive solution. Attaching the ends of a bridge is less problematic. They are set at both ends in concrete foundations on the land. Only for long bridges, which are used only on very large ponds, is an additional post support in the water needed.

GOOD TO KNOW

Tips for a Safe Step

Bridges and walkways must be at least 60 centimeters wide to be comfortably and safely usable. A railing in particular makes bridges safer. So that a railing can fulfill its function, it must be fastened securely and be at least one meter high. A wobbling railing lulls the user into false security and is sometimes more dangerous than no railing at all. When paths are connected smoothly with a bridge or walkway, no stumbling results. If steps are needed, though, they must be easily recognized, wide and deep enough to allow comfortable stepping. If small children are in the garden, walkways or bridges naturally become favorite places to play. The little adventurers like to hang their hands or feet in the water or reach for frogs or salamanders, which can lead to dangerous situations.

Sun Decks by the Pond

It is a special experience to lie on warm wooden planks and let your arm hang over the edge into the fresh, cool water. From this dry observation post one can casually and comfortably observe the light reflections on the water, the cheery activity of the dragonflies and the life in the swimming pond. Such a place for relaxation lets a vacation feeling arise purely and has a guaranteed restorative value.

Variations on a Theme

Sun decks are usually rectangular platforms made of parallel wooden laths or boards mounted at right angles to carrier beams. Through

The bigger a sun deck is, the greater is its spare-time value.

small gaps of barely a centimeter, rainwater can flow away without the feet of garden furniture getting caught in the cracks. When choosing the wood, make sure it matches the material of the walkways.

Besides classical rectangular sun decks, countless variations are possible: diverging rectangles, octagonal or round designs, sun decks with diagonal planks or inserted plant islands, and many more. In combining rectangular and round patterns, the transitions can be very tricky. Whoever has little experience in woodworking should call in a specialist here too, for a lot of wood can be wasted in cutting without producing satisfactory results.

In all designs, a stable substructure is important, so that the support posts have no direct contact with the ground and the sun deck is stable and level. So that experiencing the water is close at hand, the sun deck must not be raised too high above the water level. A deck just a few centimeters above the water also has the advantage of covering the unattractive substructure and having just the sun and not the deck reflected in the water. If a permeable special foil is laid under the deck, it prevents the growth of unwanted weeds.

Besides the spare-time value that a sun deck offers, it is also very suitable for concealing any pond technology that may be present. Access to a pump shaft under the deck is allowed by a hatch made of hinged boards. This solution avoids placing the shaft in another part of the garden near the pond.

Building a Sun Deck Yourself

Sun-deck designs resemble those of walkways that project into the water, but as a rule they are clearly wider, so as to offer much room for sunbathing and relaxing. Unlike walkways, the side of the wooden deck toward the water is placed on a wall raised barely over the water level, isolated by pond foil, and fixed with a blind board to conceal the wall.

Finished sun decks are only rarely available in the trade. The usual wooden panels measuring 0.5 by 0.5 meter are not very well suited to use for sun decks and, with their impregnated wood, contradict the idea of a natural swimming pond. Stable, comfortable and attractive sun decks consist of boards, especially moisture-resistant ones, of planed larch wood. For the substructure, foundation points of concrete with inserted screw threading are useful. A secure attachment needs a foundation point every two meters. The carrier beams (14 x 7 cm thick) are made with holes and set on the screw rods and foundation points. Nuts with flanges attached under the beams allow the carrier beams to be leveled easily. Finally the beams are attached from above with flanged nuts. This method has the advantage that if the ground settles, height correction can be made without problems.

Decks of planed, smoothed wooden boards or laths are generally laid at right angles. In attaching them from above, rust-free stainless steel bolts must be used. In this way single planks can be replaced easily if they are damaged.

Larger and wider designs require more than two parallel carrier beams. For terrace-size sun decks a box-type substructure is required. As in building walkways, the use of modular structures is recommended here. Aside from the invisible screws in the boards, the modules of a sun deck can also be laid out in checkerboard patterns, which can look very charming.

If the deck extends horizontally over the water, a carrier beam can be extended over the edge wall to avoid setting a support post in the swimming area. But since such designs make the water surface smaller, and make the water area under the deck a trap, especially for children, this solution is not highly recommended. Impregnated softwood is frequently used to build a sun deck. The modest price, easy working and universal availability favor this choice, but the wood must be replaced often.

Sitting places right by the water have a very special charm.

Whoever feels bound by ecological thoughts—and that is the case among most people who are interested in swimming ponds—can spend a little more money and strive for an esthetically impressive and also very long-lasting design by working with larch wood. Finally, just one more recommendation: Hire a specialist to do the job. Besides the saving of time and nerves, one thus acquires a stable, really good-looking sun deck.

Ladders and Stairs

Comfortable entrance and exit contribute to the complete comfort of a swimming pond. Since the swimming area as a rule is so deep that the swimmer cannot push off from the shore, climbing out of the water without a ladder or steps can often result in an unwanted tumble. It is also not everyone's style to jump into the water. Help in entering is thus really obligatory and should be planned from the start. Installing it later is complicated, since the water level must be lowered for it.

A simple ladder is the most economical and sorting solution. Available stainless steel ladders that can be attached securely to the walkway or sun deck are a good choice. Naturally, wooden ladders that are securely attached to the deck, and must have spacer shafts to a vertical wall at their lower end to assure a vertical position, match the wooden deck better.

Stairs for Access

The easier and more stable alternative to a ladder is the flight of stairs. They should be built by a specialist and fitted with a handrail. Seven steps are enough for swimming away and pushing off. After the last step, vertical boards running to the bottom of the pond supply sufficient stability. They are set in a wooden tub weighted with stones, which hinders the stairs from rising. The large area of the tub—unlike the resting points of the ladder—avoids damaging the pond foil on the bottom. At the upper end, the stairs are attached to the blind board below the deck or walkway. Since the stepping surfaces of ladders or stairs can easily become slippery from moisture, a rust-free tread attached to the upper side can prevent slipping.

Ladders to aid entrance are practical and save space.

Wooden stairs lead step by step into the swimming pond.

GOOD TO KNOW

Wood Types for Walkways, Bridges and Sun Decks

Pine:
Conifer wood often used outdoors, easy to work and relatively inexpensive. Lasts 8 to 10 years.

Larch:
Native conifer, firm, weather-resistant, medium price range, lasts 10 to 12 years. Native mountain larch is a little more expensive and lasts longer, to 15 years.

Red Cedar:
The firm reddish wood of the Canadian red cedar is very weather-resistant but relatively expensive, lasts 12 to 15 years.

Oak:
Traditional and strong native hardwood, relatively resistant outdoors, which justifies the high price. Lasts 15 to 20 years.

Locust:
Its relatively good weather resistance and hardness makes locust wood a good but almost equally expensive alternative to tropical woods. Lasts 15 to 20 years.

Eucalyptus:
In style for some years; an almost equally useful but somewhat more reasonably priced alternative to teak. Lasts 15 to 20 years.

Bangkirai:
A hard, fine-pored tropical wood from Indonesia and Malaysia, it is very durable and weathers to gray over time. Lasts 15 to 25 years. For ecological and humanitarian reasons, only tropical wood with an FSC seal, from controlled, established plantations, should be used. The same applies to other tropical woods.

Bongossi (Azobe):
A very hard, compact-fiber, heavy tropical wood that is elastic and weather-resistant. The dark brown wood, graying from weathering, is attacked by neither insects nor boring mussels and is thus a good wood for boats and structures in water. Lasts 15 to 25 years.

Teak:
Now as before, teak is the best and most weather-resistant wood, but also the most expensive, for outdoor use. It is almost indestructible. For the reasons stated above, only teak with the FSC seal, from controlled, established plantations should be used.

Both ladders and stairs must be mounted before the pond is filled. A very elegant and classy solution is access in the corner of the swimming area. This variation, though, should be built only by a specialist. Larch wood is recommended for the job, as it lasts particularly long in the water. Neither wooden ladders nor stairs are removed in winter.

Entrances made of concrete or natural stone are clearly more demanding. In addition, these materials can also become very slippery, and no satisfactory cure for this problem has been found. Thus their care is also considerably greater than that of wood.

Working with Wood

The material used most often for walkways, bridges and sun decks is wood. Only natural wood should be used. The advantages of this practical and handy, but above all good-looking building material are somewhat limited by a few disadvantages. Wet wood surfaces unavoidably

Wood is the preferred material for load-bearing structures as well as garden furniture.

become slippery. Constant contact with water, such as by the support posts of walkways, or by ladders or stairs on which one gets into the water, makes most low-priced woods rot quickly. Impregnation can delay the rotting process, but goes against the principle of the natural swimming pond. Impregnations containing bitumen are absolutely taboo. Pressure-treated wood (usually soft conifers like pine or fir) no longer gives off the salts used in impregnation into the water, according to producers' information, if they have been stored at room temperature (15 to 20 degrees C) for several weeks before use. Yet the use of such woods has been criticized, since they rank as hazardous waste when discarded. An alternative is the so-called "thermo-wood". Through heat treatment clearly over 100 degrees C, the dimensional stability of broadleaf or coniferous wood is improved. It becomes more resistant to wood-replacement processes like fungus attack and is more stable in form than untreated wood. In addition, it shows these characteristics, unlike pressure-treated wood, within the piece of work as well. Native larch wood is used most often by swimming-pond builders, as it is relatively weather-resistant without being impregnated. For all types of wood that contain tannic acid, like oak, locust, bongossi and other tropical woods, the use of stainless steel fittings is recommended.

"Artificial Wood"

Plastic-bound wooden materials, so-called wood plastic composites (WPC), are relatively new on the market. The synthetic material, composed of up to 90% wood pellets or shavings, is bound with polypropyls (PP) or polyethyls (PE) and sold in various forms. WPC is resistant to insect and fungus, rot-resistant and easy to work. It does not splinter or crack, is very easy to care for, and thanks to these characteristics is combines with tropical wood for use in pond building. One problem: As with all synthetic materials of mixed components, is disposal of scrap.

Stainless steel is a non-rusting, lasting alternative to wood. It is useful, above all, for layouts in which modern design is valued, and in which the house also includes much glass and steel.

Space to Relax and Enjoy

Terraces, sitting places, rest zones and sun decks increase the regenerative value of a swimming pond many times. One can relax and observe the life by and in the pond and the play of sunlight on the water surface from a seat on the shore. These rest zones make the swimming pond a meeting place for friends and visitors, where one can relax and enjoy a summer afternoon, chat by candlelight in the evening, or spend time alone with a good book. Sitting places and terraces expand the pond landscape optically and give it more breadth. In every case it is worthwhile to put these seats on a firm ground covering and frame them with bright plants. With comfortable garden furniture

Sitting places by the pond should be friendly, well paved, and furnished with comfortable furniture.

that contributes to the spare-time character of the scene and makes this valuable part of the garden more inviting contributes to solid comfort.

Then too, not only the warm season is suitable for social activities around the swimming pond. If it is big enough, friends can be invited in winter for ice skating or curling. Instead of cold drinks, mulled wine or punch can be served. Torches also make the garden wondrously lovely in the snowy evening landscape and invite friends from afar to the ice festival.

Terraces and Sitting Places

On warm summer days, the "outdoor living rooms", as they are often called, are simply irreplaceable. Throughout the day, sitting places and terraces offer a place to rest and sunbathe. Children find a place to play there, swimming guests can leave all kinds of utensils. From there one can step into the cool water or dry out when they climb onto the attached shore. In the evening and the night there is room for a pleasant dinner for two or for getting together with friends. In practice, they form the center of the layout, where the activities of swimmers and visitors are concentrated, and from which swimming trips into the pond can begin. Thus a locale treated gently by the sun is just right. Where the sun's rays are too hot, sunshades or awnings provide shade.

Sitting by the Water

When the terrace extends right to the water, direct experiencing of the fascinating pond world from this position is possible. Wooden terraces can even slightly overhang the water and enhance the effect of close encounters. When the swimming pond is right near the house, it is

Classic Paving Materials

Cinder Blocks have an unpretentious, rustic air. Disadvantage: In humid weather, algae settle on the porous surfaces and make them slippery.

Natural Stone Slabs are especially elegant. One can arrange them in polygonal forms or as equal plates. Unpolished surfaces have the advantage of not becoming slippery. Often-used types are granite, sandstone types and porphyry.

Artificial Paving Stones are very varied, easy to lay, universally available and easy to maintain. Unfortunately, many types look bad in natural settings. But now there are also artificial paving stones that, with irregular angles and color variations, convincingly imitate the character of natural paving stones.

Combined Natural and Artificial Paving Stones can look very good. Even the less good-looking washed concrete slabs can take on a new value in combination with natural or artificial stones. Paving stones used in combination are a possible way to create sitting places and terraces inexpensively and yet attractively.

"Soft Materials" like gravel, sand, chips or bark mulch are especially suited for light sitting places by the pond somewhat farther away from the house. The loose material expresses a closeness to nature and can form an expressive footpath material.

linked to the architecture by a terrace and then offers an all-year experience. Swimming ponds farther from the house require an "infrastructure" and thus earn their sitting places. Their permanent attachment is just as practical as that of a terrace near the house. The further the pond is from the house, the more casual it can appear. Where one places garden furniture for long periods and does not want them to wobble or sink into the ground, lasting solidifying of the soil with paving material makes sense.

Practical Terrace Planning

Sitting places can be laid out so that they follow the gentle curves of the pond shore; they can also project into the pond and almost take on the character of an island. When planning, one should be aware that water surfaces overhung by terraces drive building costs up. If the land slopes sharply, the spoil can be used to build up the sloping side so that a sitting place can be built by the water. Natural stone walls to support the slopes can be located so that terraces have room beside the pond.

What Style, What Pavement?

The style of a garden and the character of a swimming pond determine the esthetic decisions concerning the building materials. A harmonious impression is achieved when one sticks with the materials, colors and textures of the house. The more formal the garden formation is, the more strictly the forms of the paving materials for the sitting place must be. The more natural the character of the pond garden, the more rustic the ground covering for the terrace or sitting place can be. As a rule, a so-called "dry paving" suffices for the latter, laying the stones in a layer of sand that is placed on a gravel bed for better drainage. So the stones stay really firm, for example, in a terrace by the house or a strictly formal layout, it is best to lay the paving stones in a thin concrete mixture. In general, the smaller the laid stones are, the better it is to lay them in a bed of thin concrete to maintain as stable and enduringly even a pavement as possible.

Durable Paving Materials

No matter what material is chosen, the materials used must be frost-resistant and, in the case of artificial stone, also abrasion-resistant. Normal bricks are, as a rule, not winter-resistant, as water can easily penetrate their porous surface, freeze and break the brick, Hard-burned cinder blocks made for outdoor use, slate, and some other natural stones have the unwanted characteristic of having a little bit rubbed off them with every step on them. After a time there is not much left of the stone. Good sturdy natural stones are thus expensive, but the investment pays in the long run. Regionally available types of stone are usually less expensive than imported types and naturally fit into the surroundings harmoniously. Paving sitting places or terraces with wooden planks or other wood paving will be less weather-resistant. Only impregnated wood, regularly maintained,

An intimate atmosphere arises at the sitting place thanks to a frame of trees.

or expensive tropic wood will guarantee a longer life span for the materials. So they do not become slippery with moss and algae, it must often be cleaned with a brush.

Integrating Sitting Places in the Garden

Plants not only border sitting places and terraces; they also create a harmonious link with the swimming pond and garden. Flowerbeds and solitary trees play a supportive role here. Ground cover and cushion plants soften borders, high shrubs and decorative trees create a background that creates solitude and intimacy. A private atmosphere also arises when sitting places near the pond are not simply places in open areas, but are backed up by an earthen wall or dry wall.

Decoration goes along with the layout and planting. The choice of the sitting furniture is also a decisive formative criterion. If it is weather-resistant, it can stay outdoors all summer. Lasting, robust garden furniture is made of iron or steel, various hardwoods or plastic. The latter may be had for low prices but is not necessarily attractive. Spare-time furniture of wickerwork but does not withstand humid weather well. An alternative is woven furniture in which the natural material of willow or rattan is replaced by scarcely distinguishable synthetic material.

Potted plants naturally belong on any terrace. Sitting places also gain from their striking presence. When one notices the aroma, colorful flowers and fruits, especially interesting leaves or pleasant autumn colors of the potted and bedded plants on and near the terrace, they offer an added pleasure to the senses.

Integrating the Swimming Pond into the Garden

So that a swimming pond has a good effect and does not remain a foreign body in a garden, its blending into the environment is important. No matter whether a flower meadow or lawn, shrubbery or flowerbeds, a shore path or paved sitting place adjoins it, in every case, considered and careful planning around the pond matters. Squeezing a swimming pond between vegetable beds and a driveway is senseless and not only reduces the optical pleasure, but also reduces the value of the swimming water. In the end, one would like to rest in the sun after a dip in the pond and relax in pleasant surroundings.

A Question of Taste

It should be clear to all that a strictly formed designer garden does not go with a rustic country house, nor a many-colored rural garden with a modern bungalow of glass and stainless steel. The same applies to the swimming pond in the garden. Formal swimming ponds with clear geometrical shapes thus require a corresponding form of straight, functional paths and spaces that link them with the architecture of the house. Naturally formed swimming ponds with gentle shorelines, on the other hand, need flowing transitions and curving lines, so they lose none of their charm.

The swimming pond takes up the contours of its shores and the circular shape of the wooden terrace.

Although much of the planting depends on the formation, the choice of materials also takes on a decisive significance. Too many different materials, colors and structures make a disturbed impression and destroy the harmony of the layout. Using similar materials and structures for the garden, solidifying the paths and sitting places are recommended and sensible, just as in the house.

Setting Accents

In fixing the sitting place, paths and pond edges, one attains a harmonious, restful impression when, if possible, only one kind of stone is used. A second type of stone can be used to set accents.

Wooden decks walkways, and wooden plank paths, are an attractive alternative to paving the layout and go as well with a natural formation as with formal concepts. In any case, they should be resistant to slipping, which is achieved as a rule with rippled surfaces. An

attractive planting can set additional accents. Appropriate accessories include, besides sitting furniture, vases and flowerpots in particular. They can hold plants or, if they have nice shapes and surface structures, can have an effect even when empty. Several pots of similar size and shape, set up within view of each other, create optical connections and pull the layout together.

Creating Correspondences

The planting in the surroundings will succeed all the better the more one orients the shore formation to structures already present. With small groups of trees near the shore, optical correspondences with large shrubs and tree groups on the property or in the nearest neighborhood can be created. The vertical accentuating of the otherwise usually very even surroundings of the swimming pond is thus an important formative element.

Grounds on slopes allow the building of an artificial brook course that empties into the swimming pond. When the shores of the brook are formed with gravel, boulders and adequate shore planting, this is a perfect continuation of the water motif provided by the swimming pond.

Softly splashing spring and fountain stones or firmly installed wells and springs also vary the water theme and thus create a connection with the pond landscape. If you lack the technical skill to make such a layout, small barrel or trough ponds and miniature water gardens by the sitting place or on the terrace offer a charming and unproblematic alternative.

An eye-catcher can be, for example, a nice terra-cotta vase, or a pretty planting.

Attractive Shore Planting

Swimming ponds become really attractive and linked to the garden only by successful planting of the regeneration area. The shore-zone area deserves special attention; this is the immediate shoreline that borders on the open water surface. In the shallow-water areas various flowers and decorative leafy plants can be located. For a good transition to "dry land" and colorful accents, for example, you can use various swamp iris *(Iris pseudacorus, I. laevigata, I. virginica* and *I. insata),* swamp calla *(Calla palustris),* and pickerelweed *(Pontederia cordata).* They are also important as water-clearing plants and accent the line at which the shallow-water zone goes over to swamp and gravel areas. They are supported by cattails *(Typha* species), calamus *(Acorus calamus)* and other typical shallow-water plants.

In the moist shore soil, not only do such attractive flowering plants as marsh marigold *(Caltha palustris),* American skunk cabbage *(Lysichiton americanus)* and purple loosestrife *(Lythrum salicaria)* thrive, but so do numerous low or creeping plants such as swamp forget-me-not *(Myosotis palustris),* creeping Jenny *(Lysimachia nummularia)* and euphorbia *(Euphorbia palustris).* The named types are perennial plants that sprout in springtime and die back to the rootstock in autumn. In the next spring they send out fresh shoots, provided the plant is really winter-resistant. Plants that are not, but still live for several years, include white arums *(Zantedeschia aethiopica)* or paper reed *(Cyperus papyrus),* which feel as much at home in the shallow-water area as in the moist shore mud. They are best planted in pots so they can be moved easily in autumn and brought in to overwinter in a safe, a frost-free environment. Despite the extra care that they require, they enrich the layout and certainly draw admiring looks. They can overwinter with all the potted plants in a bright, frost-free space. The room temperature should be about 10 degrees C.

Shore Planting

Swamp and shoreline plants that are optimally suited for such a vegetation zone through their needs and habits are indispensable for shore planting. As a rule, these are also perennials that cause just a one-time investment that pays off over the years. Some lovely representatives like Roger's flower *(Astilboides),* Greiskraut *(Ligularia* species) and umbrella plant *(Darmera)* have large, attractive leaves that radiate an almost tropical luxuriance. Others await with delicate, grasslike leaves, including Siberian iris *(Iris sibirica),* sedge *(Carex* species) and day lilies *(Hemerocallis* hybrids). Colorful accents are set by avens *(Geum* species, primroses *(Primula* species), loosestrife *(Lysimachia* species), false spirea *(Astilbe* hybrids) and purple loosestrife. If the ground across from the pond edges is less moist (as is the case with most foil ponds), an appropriate impression can still be created by using plants like saxifrage *(Bergenia* hybrids), Roger's flower *(Rodgersia* species), ferns and hostas. The huge, strongly structured leaves of mammothleaf *(Gunnera manicata)* and Chinese

Edging beds with lots of variation form a stylish frame for the swimming pond.

113

Day Lily (*Hemerocallis hybrids*)
Daylilies are very winter-tough, and most can stand in full sun all day. Partial shaded is recommended only for the types with glowing colors, so the flowers do not fade. Several hundred types in all colors are available in the trade. Flower size and growth height vary.

Golden Groundsel (*Ligularia dentata 'Desdemona'*)
These winter-resistant perennials come from mild Europe and Asia. They grow best in moist soil at a protected place in full sun. Growth occurs through division in the spring. The 'Desdemona' type has big violet-tinged leaves and orange flowers.

Toad Lily (*Tricyrtis hirta*)
The toad lily is much better looking than its name suggests. It is really a pretty, rhizome-forming perennial with nice colors and designs. The winter-resistant plants need a sheltered semi-shaded location with moist, deep soil.

Joe-Pye-Weed (*Eupatorium purpureum*)
Joe-Pye-weed is a leafy perennial coming from North America, with leaves that smell like vanilla. It grows up to two meters high and also ranks among the medicinal herbs. It grows best in a soil that brings water in full sun or partial shade.

rhubarb *(Rheum palmatum)* are striking. These leafy perennials have a great long-distance effect and should be planted only where they have plenty of place to unfold. The same applies to large grasses such a pampas grass *(Cortaderia selloana)* or Chinese reed *(Miscanthus* species). They not only attain enormous size. Grasses like foxtail *(Pennisetum)*, panic grass *(Panicum virgatum)*, reedy grass *(Phalaris arundinacea* var. *picta)* or moor grass *(Molinia)* are indispensable components of shore planting, for their stalks that rustle softly in the wind and their filigreed growths are very charming. Special care, though, is needed for bamboo. The underground runners are very invasive and sometimes push their points through the pond foil. A rhizome guard can prevent the worst.

The Art of Flowerbed Formation

Successful planting is not always an easy task for the layman. The art consists of laying out the bed so all the plants look good, harmonize with each other in color—or create inspiring contrasts—and the beds look inviting all through the garden season. An interplay of some decorative shrubs that must not be too big or grow too quickly, with flowers and leafy perennials such as ferns, grasses and annuals forms the ideal mixture for a varied shore planting that looks good all year.

Decorative Shrubs on the Shore

The use of decorative shrubs on the shore of a swimming pond must be dome with caution. Quickly growing trees and shrubs, such as most willows, black alders or birches may only be planted some distance from the pond. They not only shade the whole pond very quickly and contribute their fallen leaves and, in particular, catkins and fruits as unwanted nutrients in the pond water, but their roots can also damage the pond foil in time. Removing a well-rooted willow from the vicinity of the sensitive foil of a swimming pond is very difficult and should therefore be avoided from the start. Planting conifers in the shore area is a matter of taste, but not necessarily recommended, since many kinds become very dominant in a short time and oppress any other plants.

Slowly growing rhododendron types and azaleas *(Rhododendron)*, Japanese maple *(Acer palmatum* 'Dissectum')*,* and numerous flowering shrubs like deutzia *(Deutzia)*, spiraea *(Spiraea)*, beauty bush *(Kolkwitzia)*, ninebark *(Physocarpus)* and snowball types *(Viburnum* species), that prefer not overly dry soils, are well suited. They can be kept to a certain size by strong trimming without suffering from it. For the natural shoreline, some dogwood varieties (such as *Cornus alba* 'Sibirica'), that grow to a modest height, are suitable.

Perennials for the Edge of the Swimming Pond

The beds on the shore can be formed especially colorfully and permanently with perennials. An outstanding role is played by perennials that are mostly high-growing, striking types with splendid flowers or dominant habits. They set the standards and draw the attention. Usually a few examples are enough to create the desired effect. Typical examples for the pond rim are meadow rue *(Thalictrum)*, Joe-Pye-weed *(Eupatorium)*, the large types of groundsel *(Ligularia przewalskii, L. dentate)*, false spirea *(Astilbe thunbergii* and *A. x Arendsii* hybrids) and day lilies *(Hemerocallis* hybrids). These primary performers dominate the accompanying plants that remain smaller, have less eye-catching flowers and are planted in greater numbers, often in groups. In shore formation, for example, medium-height loosestrife types *(Lysimachia)*, Japanese anemones *(Anemone japonica)*, meadowsweet *(Filipendula vulgaris)*, spiderwort *(Tradescantia andersoniana* hybrids, waxbells *(Kirengeshoma palmate)* and avens *(Geum coccineum, G. rivale* and hybrids) play this role. So-called full perennials with small flowers or pillow-like growth help to fill in holes, harmonize transitions, and are also suitable for the edge of a border. These plants, mostly ground cover, take on an important task in shore planting: They help to establish edges and enclosures such as foil strips. Typical full perennials for shore formation are bugle *(Ajuga reptans)*, knotweed *(Persicaria bistorta)*, and creeping Jenny *(Lysimachia nummularia)*, as well as the various geranium species.

Moor Beds

Where enough space is available on the shore, it is worth putting in a moor bed. Turf is used here as a substratum. Homeless plants such as toad lilies *(Tricyrtis hirta),* sundew *(Drosera* species) and pitcher plants *(Sarracenia* species) find a home here, as do heaths *(Eerica* and *Calluna* types). Deer fern *(Blechnum spicant)* and dwarf rhododendron types. The slim-leafed cotton grass *(Eriophorum angustifolium)* also thrives in the constantly damp soil of a moor bed, and looks striking with its wadded seed clusters when it can form large groups. Because the milieu of a moor bed is acidic while the swimming pond is rather basic, a division of the two zones with a foil barrier is necessary. Bizarre roots or dead-tree stumps make striking decorations. Moss and lichen settle on them and do their part to create the total effect of the layout.

White arum (Zantedeschia aethiopica) is a pleasant beauty that must overwinter free of frost.

Japanese anemone (Anemone japonica hybrids) also bloom in partial shade.

Paths by the Pond

To be able to know the fascinating world of a swimming pond intimately, with all its plants and animals, paths must follow the shore. They not only allow safe walking and make maintenance easier, but when properly made, they also accentuate the border between pond and garden visibly without really separating them.

The naturally planted shore area with curving bays requires the paths to match it. Free-swinging paths with a (soft) foundation, such as gravel paths, always work better than straight concrete or regular artificial stone pavement. Sharply defined angles and crass transitions are to be avoided when possible. An attractive, pleasant path foundation can be made of individual stepping stones of natural stone, between which grass or creeping ground cover can grow. Wood pavement and wooden sills are only suitable conditionally, since they become slippery when wet and can become a safety risk.

Lights in the open can add a stylistic accent.

Step Safely on the Shore

Not only on wood surfaces, but on all paths in the shore area, safety comes first. Foil ponds have the great advantage that the ground beyond the foil is usually dry and not swampy. Thus paths can come right to the edge of the water without sagging or gradually sinking. If individual steps or stepping stones led into the water, they would have to be well supported by a substructure. Here it makes sense to include possible stepping stones in the plans from the start. Paths on damp shores can be stabilized by installing corner stones or concrete slabs. The bordering watertight area of the pond should likewise be established. Visible foils do not look good, and they are also damaged by weather and by mechanical injuries.

Evening Light Play

Since a pond also has its charm in the evening or night, lighting the paths by the shore makes sense. Whoever cannot bring in a specialist to lay the electric cables can turn to low-voltage systems. Solar lamps that are equipped with a ground wire in the soil are a simple alternative. Weak lamps also give out enough light in the evening to assure that an evening excursion does not end in an unwilling bath. They also have the advantage in that

One can explore the surroundings of the pond sure of foot on stepping stones.

the animals by the pond are not irritated by the artificial source of light.

Underwater Lighting

Very lovely effects can be created at the pond in the evening with underwater lights. The installation of the lights can be done in the regeneration area, where the light shines through the underwater plants. They can also be attached to the walls of the swimming area, but this must be considered when planning so appropriate niches for the lights can be made.

Only spotlights with low voltage (maximum 12 volts) are allowed in the water. They are therefore connected to a transformer that must be located in a safe place. The installation should be done so that the light is not blinding, but always turned aside from the sun deck or sitting place on the shore.

Spotlights installed underwater make the pond catch the eye at night too.

More light can be produced by using halogen lights. They have the pleasant side effect of needing less energy. The future surely belongs to light diodes that can create color effects, such as the glass-fiber technology. There a source of light outside the water is directed along glass fibers into the water. As colorful and beautiful as these lights are, they are still very expensive at this time.

GOOD TO KNOW

Stepping stones in the Pond

Stepping stones placed in the shoreline zone of the swimming pond need a secure foundation so that they do not sag or wobble when stepped on. It is best to plan the stepping stones before the pond is lined with foil, since it is difficult to put in the foundations later.

As first a concrete foundation is poured on a bed of gravel. A padding fleece between the concrete foundation and the foil prevents damage to the foil when the mount is built. On the laid foil a mount is now built up to just under the future water level with watertight wall bricks (hard-burned cinder blocks) and mortar. Then the stepping stone is mortared to the top. If it hangs over the mount somewhat, one does not see the substructure after the water is put in. In any case, the stepping stones must be big enough—at least 45 x 45 centimeters—and firmly anchored so that once can stand on them safely. The gap between the stepping stones must not be more than 35 to 40 centimeters, so that one can step easily.

Creating Transitions

The swimming pond in the garden appears less strange than a conventional pool because of its natural formation. To blend the body of water nicely into the surroundings and create a harmonious connection between pond and garden, successful transitions between the water and the "dry land" are especially important. A swimming pond looks best when it is not only surrounded by a cared-for but bare grass or gravel surface, but also when variously formed realms alternate. To achieve a pleasant approach, one must naturally keep the entrance to the swimming basin mostly free of plants, while the regeneration area in the shallow-water zone can be enclosed by a protective belt of various shoreline plants.

A row of stepping stones links the solid and liquid elements.

Between the Elements

Many damp-soil plants like meadowsweet *(Filipendula ulmaria),* sedge *(Carex),* anf primroses also feel at home in the wet ground of the swamp zone. They can be planted either in the permanently wet area or outside the pond in regular garden soil. If one makes use of their ambivalent character in formation, the border between the elements disappears and a harmonious transition is created.

Animals find refuge in the areas dominated by vegetation, while the open areas by the water invite guests such as birds, butterflies and dragonflies; observing them becomes a special pleasure. Graveled, almost plantless shore zones that alternate with zones of shore vegetation also allow one's gaze to sweep over the water surface. Individual large boulders set optical accents and also offer birds a place to rest and observe. When possible, such chunks of rock or boulders should consist of local types of stone and also appear in other parts of the garden.

In shore formation it should always be remembered that all planted areas must be reachable for maintenance.

Also worth considering is the time one would like to spend on maintenance. Where constant pinching, trimming and tying must be done, the fun soon disappears from the green world.

Dry Walls by the Pond

An especially attractive solution to a transition consists of piling up the soil dug out of the pond pit on one of the pond's shores and holding it with a dry wall. On property with a slope, part of the slope can simultaneously be secured and more space provided for a rest zone by the swimming pond. Dry walls are built of stone chunks on a gravel bed without using mortar. As a rule, they are not more than one meter high. Having the wall face southward is practical, so that it can absorb as much of the sun's warmth as possible and save it until the evening hours. Thus it becomes a valuable biotope for small animals. An attractive planting involves primarily cushion and rock-garden perennials such as stonecrops, houseleek, saxifrage types and cushion phlox. The side of the dry wall turned toward the pond can be planted with small shrubs and thus lead into the garden behind it without being seen as a foreign body. So that soil and nutrients are not carried into the pond by erosion, a planted buffer zone of some two meters or a sitting place between the dry wall and the water makes sense. Since such extensive excavating and stacking to make a secure dry wall are very demanding for the layman, it is best to call in a garden-building firm.

Dry walls by swimming ponds can absorb the sun's warmth and store it, as long as they face south.

Decorations on the Shore

Garden decoration is becoming more and more popular and can also add value to the surroundings of a swimming pond. From planted bowls to spring or fountain stones to artistically created sculptures of artificial stone or cast bronze, anything is possible. Individual decorations make sitting places by the pond more inviting and create colorful accents in the flower-deficient phases of the garden year. With all the joy in decoration, though, one is well advised not to lose the natural character of the swimming pond and its surroundings. In case of doubt, this means finding a different place to set up a prized object and keeping the shore area of the swimming pond as authentic and natural as it is.

Fountains, Spring and Well Stones

Water in motion can be a fascinating completion to the plain, quiet surface of a swimming pond. Fountains, spring and well stones affect the senses with their soft gurgling and reflect light onto the pearly waters. To really be able to enjoy them, water plays are installed as close as possible to favorite sitting places. Simple, clear concepts fit into the natural environment of a swimming pond better in most cases than artificial compositions. With present-day pond technology, the water plays are driven by the central (and only) pump. For technology-free ponds they are fed by small electric pumps, the installation of which is best left, for reasons of safety, to the specialist.

Pots, Bowls and Vases

With relatively simple means, pots, bowls or vases can be attractive eye-catchers. With sufficient size or grouped to make small ensembles, they can also be noticed from a distance. Simple, strongly expressive forms fit best into the concept of the swimming pond. The vessels can be planted or adorned with decorative objects like shells, gravel or glass marbles. Often, though, they impress simply with their shape and structure. If the surface takes on a rustic patina in time, this can even increase the charm of the objects. Only frost-resistant objects may spend the winter outdoors, but they too can be broken if water gathers in them and expands when it freezes.

Springs stones break up the monotony along the shore.

Decorative elements can make simple spots more interesting.

Striking rocks accentuate the shore of this swimming pond. They blend with the equally striking tree shapes in the background.

Plastics and Sculptures

Slim birds, dreaming dwarfs or slumbering elves of bronze on the pond shore; amphorae, cones or balls of glazed or unglazed terra cotta beside the sitting place by the pond, or a stone nymph shyly hiding among the leaves of the shore plants—the choice of sculptures and other plastic objects as garden decorations is overwhelming. Along with the objects on sale in building stores, mail-order catalogs and specialty shops, there are also individual works made by artists that can catch the eye at the right spot on the pond shore. Reasonably priced and easy to put up are figures of painted wood or sheet metal. Mounted on spikes, they can simply be stuck in the ground. Ceramic and artistic shops offer a good place to get a look at what is offered in garden art and make contacts. The prerequisites for the long life of an often expensive garden decoration are course, a certain stability, good weather-resistance and tipping- and theft-free mounting. Striking leafy plants like Roger's flower, decorative rhubarb, ferns or grasses are the right partners for dominant sculptures. More elegant figures need a certain free space, so as not to be overwhelmed by the neighboring vegetation.

Natural Works of Art

Art and nature blend smoothly when, for example, bizarrely shaped roots, a bundle of willow withes, stone blocks affected by weather or other discovered things are set in a special place on the shore of a swimming pond. Even homemade mobiles and combinations of plant parts, feathers, snail shells and animal bones conjure up mythical themes. A bed of countless small sea shells and driftwood smoothed by the sea water and bleached by the sun can awaken maritime associations on a pond shore. Whoever walks open-eyed through nature finds enough inspirations to enrich the surroundings of the swimming pond decoratively with striking things from nature.

Check List: Safety Around the Pond

Even a puddle can be dangerous for small children. Thus, *small children should never play unsupervised in a garden in which there is a body of water.*

A complete, enclosing fence around the pond and any bridges or walkways prevents children from falling into the water and drowning.

Wooden planks of paths and walkways easily become slippery after rain or in humid weather. **Steps with rippled surfaces offer more stepping safety**. Ladders and stairs made of wood that ease entry into the swimming pond naturally become slippery in time. Add a **no-skid panel of rippled stainless steel** to prevent this.

Bridges and walkways can be made safer with **railings**. A stable attachment is important. A wobbly railing is sometimes more dangerous than none at all, because it gives the visitor a false sense of safety.

Stepping stones placed in or by the water must be attached firmly to their mounts, so that a visit to the pond does not end with an unwilling bath.

If the swimming pond is to be used in the evening, **lighting of the approach and the entry area** makes for safe swimming pleasure. **Underwater lighting** in the pond is another possible way to remove some danger from evening or nighttime swimming.

Electric installations must be made carefully and expertly. **Cables and wires must be isolated** from moisture and protected from mechanical damage (for example, from digging). Water and electricity are a dangerous mixture. Cables and wires should be installed only by experts and be thoroughly tested for safety before being put into use. **Pumps, skimmers and other electric technical devices, and all outdoor lights, must bear the VDE, TU"V or GS safety seal** to avoid the danger of a shock.

Several popular **garden plants** are poisonous, others have thorns or prickers. For example, giant bear-claw *(Heracleum mantegazzianum)*, wormwood and spurges give off a poison when touched that, together with sunlight, can cause skin irritation similar to burns.

Safety by the pond also means safety for the pond. **Pond foil** is only lasting and fulfilling its function when it is not damaged by weather conditions. Sunlight makes exposed foil brittle. In winter the sensitive material can be damaged if the ice cannot expand on at least two sides of the pond. This is true of almost every pond. Ice-pressure cushions that can be mounted on the water surface offer added protection but are scarcely needed in practice.

In pond care, the tools one uses such as shears to cut back underwater plants, or underwater scythes, must be handled carefully, so the pond foil is not damaged.

When **cleaning** stepping stones or walkways, **chemicals should be avoided**. They damage or destroy the biological balance in the swimming pond if they spill into the water by accident. A thorough brushing with clear water generally suffices to clean wood or natural stone. In stubborn cases, a high-pressure cleaner helps, but it too can be used only with clear water without detergents.

A Heart For Nature

Swimming ponds with their variety of plant and animal life offer a wonderful opportunity to observe the processes of nature closely and help one learn to understand them. Even pond owners whose previous interest was not primarily in nature may also lie suddenly on a walkway and look intently into the mysterious depth of the water, for when nature moves into the swimming pond, their curiosity about the life in and by the water is awakened.

Open Yourself to Nature

People who have decided on a swimming pond show by their choice of a natural body of swimming water that they have a heart for nature. They turn away from the belief that technology can control all life processes perfectly, and they let nature take over a part of the rule. They are richly rewarded for it—everyday wonders that are revealed only to those who are ready to look and open themselves to nature with all their senses. The growth of plants, the beauty of their flowers, but also the wilting and passing at the end of a season are important and interesting experiences that often fade out of the picture in the everyday world dominated by speed and greed, stress and technology. For children in particular, it means an important experience to be able to observe the development of life closely. And where does it go better than by and in the water, in which all life once originated? The growing of animals, the flight of a dragonfly, the development of a frog out of a tiny tadpole, for example, are an exciting drama every year So is the wonderful development of the pond flora in spring, when in the first warm days the world in the water and its surroundings suddenly becomes green.

Even when advertising wants us to believe that summer never ends and the sun always shines, we know exactly that in nature there are also gray days, and that the wilting of vegetation in autumn and the cold, dark winter exist. But then too, one can still find life in and by the water, maintaining itself in niches and hanging on until spring when it comes to new life. The pond teaches us that saying good-bye in autumn may hurt, but after a cold winter nature awakens to new life. Following such yearly cycles is more exciting than any novel, for it takes place daily before our eyes, by and in our swimming pond!

Right: *Pure idyll—one who calls such a rustic bath-house his own can count himself lucky.*

Left: *The luxuriant plant life by this pond is continued in the greening of the house front with climbing plants.*

Understanding Natural Cycles

In the building of a swimming pond, more than that of other artificial ponds, numerous environmental factors must be considered so that the water quality will be good and thus fit to swim in, and will stay that way for the duration. Forward-looking planning and regular checking are, along with certain maintenance, prerequisites for the success of a swimming-pond project. Naturally the layman wonders, in view of the apparently complex technology, why puddles and pools in the woods do not stink badly, and why naturally formed ponds invert only in exceptional cases although nobody looks after them. The answer is relatively simple: In nature, quiet standing bodies of water like ponds and pools are created where the required conditions exist. Where the prerequisites for a natural pond no longer exist, these bodies of water disappear.

Children are interested in everything that lives in the swimming pond. It is good if you can explain it to them!

Artificially made ponds, on the other hand, are often placed where people want them for esthetic reasons. They should look the same over long periods of time, make a certain impression and correspond to a foreordained concept of use—for example, as a fish, decorative or swimming pond. There is also the condition that the pond bottom is isolated by foil and cut off from ground water and the exchange of ground gases. The system of such an artificial body of water is thus more vulnerable than a naturally created liquid biotope that can develop over a long period. Small disturbances of the ecosystem over a long period can have grave effects in an artificially created pond. In order to be able to understand the complex relationships that keep the varied systems of standing waters in existence, one must observe the natural cycles closely and try to understand them.

Living-space Swimming Pond

The inflationary concept "eco-" used at this time, under which almost everything seems to be marketed, originally comes from Greece. There *oikos* means nothing more than "house" or "housekeeping". The German natural scientist Erich Haeckel introduced the concept of "ecology" in 1866; in plain German it means "the theory of housekeeping". He used it to designate all the science of the relationships of organisms to the world around them.

In biology, ecology means the study of the reciprocal relations between individual organisms and their environment. Only when this relationship between organism and environment forms a closely sealed net of relationships that is somewhat balanced despite possible variations will it form an ecosystem that has a lasting existence. Unlike a conventional pool where the water is kept "clean", meaning clinically pure, by means of chemicals, in an ideal case an ecosystem is formed in a swimming pond in which a variety of mechanical, biological and chemical processes take place. At closer observation it becomes clear that this swimming-pond system is influenced by many factors. Above all, there is the water itself and its pH value, but also gases, minerals and thus nutrients. Sunlight, air and water temperature—nod not least, plants and animals. For good water quality, the processes that go on in the swimming-pond ecosystem must form a stable cycle. The larger the pond is, the greater the variety of types will be—and thus the probability of a balanced, well-functioning ecosystem also grows. But this does not mean that a stable balance cannot also form in small ponds.

Prerequisites for a Stable Cycle

Sunlight causes the water plants—in technical speech, also called producers—to create oxygen through photosynthesis and liberate it. In the process, they take carbon dioxide out of the water. The microscopically small algae also need sunlight for their development, and they too release oxygen through photosynthesis. They are present in every pond and are an important link in the food chain, since they serve as nutrients for water snails, water fleas, insects and their larvae, plus tiny animals like wheel, sun and slipper creatures (the so-called zooplankton). By the zooplankton in turn, small crablike creatures (Copepoda) are fed; they are eaten by insect larvae and other water dwellers. Smaller insect larvae are eaten by larger ones.

All of these animals are also plant and algae eaters—thus called consumers in the technical terminology—and give off carbon dioxide, which is necessary for plants and algae to live. When plants and plant eaters die, they sink to the bottom of the water, where they are taken apart, thus mineralized, by fungi and bacteria— in technical terms, reducers. The remains, called detritus, play an important role as "intermediate layers" for nutrients from rotting and decaying processes. The mineralized nutrients and the carbon dioxide released in this process are again processed by the producing plants. If this cycle functions, then the pond also functions.

The more varied the vegetation, the better it can do its job as a clearing establishment.

Above: *The bright green leaf frog is a rare guest in a swimming pond.*

Right: *damselflies mating, known as "wheeling."*

Below: *Yellow-rimmed beetles are feared robbers. If they turn up in large numbers, they can be fished out and resettled.*

Pond Dwellers and Guests

But back to the fauna: In and around the swimming pond "tragedies" take place daily, a constant eating and being eaten, even though man can only see a fraction of them with the naked eye. Insects and their larvae are a preferred food to all the amphibians living in the pond, who in their larval state as tadpoles are on the menu of, for example, dragonfly and beetle larvae. Despite the ruthlessness in the fight for survival, scenes full of harmony and beauty are more commonly viewed. Salamanders in their mating play, splendid dragonflies resting in the sun or pleasantly bathing songbirds in the shallow water of the shore area draw the viewer's attention to themselves.

Birds are to be seen not necessarily as inhabitants, but rather as guests in the swimming-pond ecosystem. On their visits to the water, they snap at insects or frogs and also catch one or another salamander. At the same time, they carry new life to the water in their feathers, such as eggs and larvae of various kinds of animals, and naturally also numerous plant seeds—and not least, the apparently omnipresent duckweed is carried from pond to pond by the feathered guests.

In an intact food chain, the reciprocal process between plants and bacteria, plant eaters and meat eaters, plus inorganic nutrients proceeds smoothly and without stopping in the summer months. One must not neglect to note factors the layman regards as unimportant or does not notice at all.

How the Ecosystem is Weakened

Mineral salts dissolved in the water, the classic plant nutrients that are also described as fertilizers when in concentrated form, promote, when they receive enough light, not only the growth of underwater plants, but also that of algae. They expand explosively under certain conditions—the water is colored green [p. 132] and then becomes clouded. This happens particularly often in a quick increase of water temperature in the spring, which is accompa-

Sparrows, like other songbirds, are welcome guests in the pond.

nied by powerful sunshine and a sharp increase in the pH value of the water. The masses of algae thus become a danger for the other pond inhabitants—and not least, for themselves. For the more strongly the algae multiply, the less light reaches the bottom of the pond. As a result, the underwater plants die for lack of light and disintegrate. With the decomposition of the dead plant material, oxygen released in the water is consumed and poisonous decay gas (methane) is released. Without a new oxygen supply, the animals in the pond die after the plants do. Besides the dead plant material, rotting animal cadavers give off more methane gas into the water and hasten the poisoning process. The water becomes a sewer. One can hinder this devilish cycle by partially shading the water surface. Floating plants and floating-leaf plants decrease the sunlight and thus slow the algae growth. In addition, oxygen-forming plants can compete with the algae for nutrients and hinder their massive multiplication. The zooplankton common in healthy pond water is also important. This destroys algae to such an extent that a collapse is avoided. In the nutrient-poor water of a properly planned swimming pond a mass increase of algae is thus almost impossible.

Floating leaves of pondweed (Potamogeton species).

GOOD TO KNOW

Defining Factors for Ecological Balance

Seek the optimal location for the swimming pond.

Be sure the depth of the water along the shore is sufficient. The deeper the water, the more slowly it warms on hot summer days.

Water exchange between the border and the swimming zone must be assured at any time.

In the border zones, about half of the water surface must be shaded by floating-leaf plants.

Underwater plants are the most important oxygen producers and must always be present in sufficient numbers. As a rule of thumb, 30% of the plants in the pond must be water plants.

Died-off plant parts and fallen autumn leaves should be removed from the pond before they rot and give off their nutrients to the pond water.

Fish and turtles do not belong in the swimming pond, since their metabolic products drastically worsen the water quality.

Plant-protecting means and fertilizer, plus chemical material, are absolutely forbidden in the swimming pond and the surrounding area.

The Older, the Lovelier

A newly built swimming pond looks somewhat bare at first. Between the plants of the shoreline zone and those of the shore area there are still big gaps, and the underwater and floating-leaf plants can scarcely be seen. But this changes within a few weeks, for the plants soon begin to spread and fill in the gaps. When the water lilies have established themselves, they develop not only leaves, but also a host of attractive flowers that attract attention. In two years at the most, the greenery is so thick that the border between the pond and garden can scarcely be seen. Only in the swimming zone is, now as before, the foil covering visible; on the shore, in an ideal case, it is completely covered by vegetation.

Attractive All Year

The more effectively the surroundings have been formed and planted, the better the swimming pond fits into the garden. One is well advised to provide plants that are attractive all year round, so that even in winter there will be eye-catching scenes. For example, evergreen plants and decorative shrubs with interesting habits are helpful, as are nicely colored barks and attractive decorative grasses with dry blades that are decorated with frost in cold weather.

Naturally, not every layout is perfect from the start. Even the expert cannot always evaluate the conditions on the scene correctly from the start. Usually it becomes evident only through observation over a long period, and the practical use of the swimming water, what decisions must be made and where what can be planted.

Sooner or later many plants that have grown too large, and others that are suffering where they are, need to be moved. No garden, no swimming pond is a static scene. But that is just what makes it such an interesting part of our environment and a standing challenge. Individual examples of swimming ponds that have existed for years already show clearly how beautifully they have meanwhile blended into the environment, and how attractive such a body of water becomes when it is several years old.

A grown-up swimming pond scarcely gives any clues as to its artificial origin.

Plants In and Around the Pond

A swimming pond without plants is unthinkable. Most important, of course, are those water plants that provide a smooth functioning of the system. Additional water plants, added primarily for their decorative value, such as water lilies, water arums or pickerelweed increase the optical charm of the pond and support the underwater plants that are especially active in the process of regeneration. The more striking floating-leaf plants and the swamp- or shore-zone plants in the shore area link the swimming pond perfectly with the garden and, along with spirited plantings in the nearer environs of the pond, can strengthen the natural impression.

Plants for Various Areas

Among the water plants that are necessary for the survival of a swimming pond, one differentiates among underwater plants, floating plants, floating-leaf plants and shore-zone plants. They all have important roles in the natural development of a swimming pond, which they can fulfill only when their unique needs in terms of nutrients, water depth and temperature are met. Damp-soil plants such as *Ligularia* species, meadowsweet *(Filipendula)* or the imposing ornamental rhubarb *(Gunnera manicata),* that will grow in ordinary gardens but bear a high degree of ground moisture or

Suitable plants like snakeweed (Persicaria bistorta) thrive on the shore.

even need it to thrive, link the pond vegetation with the rest of the garden and thus create an ideal transition.

Underwater plants

All plants whose leaves grow at least partly under the water surface are classed as underwater plants (submerged macrophytes). Some, like milfoil *(Myriophyllum spicatum)* form their leaves under the water surface and their flower stalks rise up out of the water. They are, of course, anchored to the soil by roots, but take in the main part of their nutrients through their leaves. Often of unlikely appearance, they yet belong to the most active oxygen producers. In addition, the green carpet of their leaves prevents too-strong algae development and excessive warming of the water on the bottom of the pond, and offers amphibians, insects and other pond residents a shelter. Therefore underwater plants are absolutely necessary in a swimming pond and should make up at least 30% of the total plant population in the pond. It is best to plant several different varieties at intervals from each other in a water depth between 50 and 100 centimeters. Most members of this plant group are very happy to spread. Many, such as the Canadian pondweed *(Elodaea Canadensis)*, expand extremely well. All underwater plants must be thinned now and then, which takes nutrients out of the pond and thus slows the growth of algae.

Floating Plants

Plants that float in the water with no ground contact are called floating plants. They drift through the pond or on its surface practically without limits. Native types such as water soldiers *(Stratiotes aloides)* are winter-resistant as a rule and dive into deep-water zones as temperatures sink, coming to the surface the following spring. Exotic types such as water lettuce *(Pistia stratiotes)* are usually not frost-resistant and must be removed in autumn and overwintered at a temperature of at least 10 degrees C. Otherwise they die at the first frost and sink to the pond bottom, where they rot and thus release superfluous nutrients into the pond.

Water Lily Hybrid *Nymphaea 'Masaniello'.*

Water Lily Hybrid *Nymphaea 'Marliacea Albida'.*

Water lily *Nymphaea odorata 'Sulphurea'*

Cape Water Lily *Nymphaea capensis.*

Floating-leaf Plants

A pond should always be at least one-third shaded. An elegant method of attaining this is by using floating-leaf plants, such as water lilies. Their leaves that lie on the water surface shade the water underneath. Unlike the floating plants, like the hornwort *(Ceratophyllum demersum)*, floating-leaf plants are rooted in the pond bottom and let their leaves ascend to the surface. They can even out small variations in the water surface with their leaves.

Water Lilies

The queen of the pond is undoubtedly the water lily *(Nymphaea* species). These impressive plants prefer warm, sunny places and deeper, muddier substrata than other water plants. In summer they develop large, attractive flowers that, as a rule, last four days before they sink again. There are not as many types and varieties of any other water plant. The native white water lily *(N. alba)* and its descendants are usually completely winter-resistant and can overwinter in ponds that are deep enough so that they do not freeze down to the bottom. As a rule of thumb: If the water lily grows in a water depth of more than 70 centimeters, it is safe from freezing. Exotic types from tropical and subtropical areas must, after their summer performance, be removed from the pond in autumn and overwintered frost-free. This also applies to all water lilies that grow in meager water depths and whose rhizomes could therefore freeze. It is most sensible to set such plants in mesh pots, which are available in the trade for this purpose. Then the roots have sufficient space, and it is easy to lift the pots in autumn along with the plants. One then puts them in a sufficiently large water container and keeps them cool but frost-free (between 5 and 8 degrees C) and not too dark until spring. The short-stemmed underwater leaves must never be completely dry. Water lilies from the shallow-water area, which root in the pond bottom, must be dug out carefully before winter begins and planted in a tub with soil. After flooding the tub, they should be overwintered in a cool but frost-free, not-too-dark place.

The velvety leaf rosettes of water lettuce (Pistia stratiotes) move freely on the water surface.

Reviving Lazy-Blooming Water Lilies

Older stands of water lilies can cover great areas of a pond with their floating leaves, but they are really lazy bloomers if they are not thinned. Thus every few years one takes up the rhizomes carefully and cuts off the rhizome tips with the shoot buds. Only these are planted in the pond again afterward.

According to their type, water lilies thrive at different water depths. It is best to learn the optimal plant depth before buying them, as well as the needs of the various types. There are very decorative types that get by with a meager water depth of between 20 and 40 centimeters, also strongly growing types whose leaves cover several square meters of water surface and need a water depth between 50 and 90 centimeters. No water lilies should be planted more than a meter deep, since the water at the lower depths warms too slowly in spring and thus delays the development of the plants. In deeper pond zones one can attain the right plant depth by setting the plant baskets on appropriately high blocks.

GOOD TO KNOW

Water Lilies for Swimming Ponds

Type	Color	Width cm	Water Depth cm
White Water Lily (*Nymphaea alba*)	white	150-200	50-90
Blue Egyptian Water Lily (*Nymphaea caerulea*)	light blue, fragrant	250-300	30-50
Cape Water Lily (*Nymphaea capensis*)	light blue	150-250	30-60
Nymphaea odorata 'Sulphurea'	sulfur yellow	120	30-45
Dwarf Water Lily (*Nyumphaea tetragona*)	white	25-40	15-40
Nymphaea tetragona 'Helvola'	light yellow	60	15-25
Nymphaea Hybrid 'Aurora'	variable copper red	75	30-60
Nymphaea Hybrid 'Blue Star'	medium blue	120-200	30-60
Nymphaea Hybrid 'Escarboucle'	vermilion	150	50-90
Nymphaea Hybrid 'Froebelii'	blood red, fragrant	90	15-30
Nynmphaea Hybrid 'Gladstoniana'	white	150-250	50-90
Nymphaea Hybrid 'James Brydon'	dark rose red	120	30-45
Nymphaea Hybrid 'Laydekeri Fulgens'	burgundy red	150	30-45
Nymphaea Hybrid 'Marliacea Albida'	white	120	30-45
Nymphaea Hybrid 'Masaniello'	rose red	150	30-60
Nymphaea Hybrid 'Virginalis'	white, fragrant	120	30-45

Edge-Zone Plants

In shallow-water and shoreline areas the so-called edge-zone plants grow. Many need meager water depths to thrive; others also grow in (swampy) ground saturated with water. They frame the water in natural ponds and surround it with continual vegetation. When planting the edge-zone plants, it is especially important to note the water depth preferred by that type of plant. Many prefer a meager depth of two to three centimeters; others tolerate a water depth of up to 30 centimeters. Especially in the case of robust, strongly growing types like cattails *(Typha* species), it must be assured that they do not damage the pond foil with their sometimes

Various types of cattails (Typha species) are a good alternative to reeds.

aggressive runners. Plant boxes closed at the bottom offer a certain protection. Along with the winter-resistant types, exotic varieties like paper reed *(Cyperus papyrus)* or the bizarre golden club *(Orontium aquaticum)* can be planted. So as not to lose them to frost, one plants them in baskets that are dug out in autumn and over-wintered frost-free.

Damp-Ground Plants

Besides the plants growing in the pond and the immediate shore area, the so-called damp-ground plants are important links with the surrounding garden landscape. The plants of this group, such as Siberian iris *(Iris sibirica),* globe flowers *(Trollius* species), primroses *(Primula* species) or golden ray (*Ligularia* species), take root in normal garden soil, but also stand or need moist to very moist substrata. In sunny places it is therefore important always to assure sufficiently high soil moisture, as the plants will otherwise suffer or wilt.

About Reeds

And here is a warning: Reeds *(Phragmites australis)* have nothing to lose in a swimming pond. This rhizome-forming grass is, to be sure, well suited to be a clearing plant and is also used for this purpose in large plant clearing areas. But because it spreads so aggressively and can puncture the pond foil with its meter-long shoots, one should never plant reeds in a swimming pond. . A better alternative consists of the various types of cattails *(Typha* species) and grass-like growths like calamus *(Acorus calamus)*, sedges *(Carex* species) or rushes *(Binse* species).

Native Plants

When using exotic, not winter-resistant plants in a pond, one should be cautions and restrained. Preparation for the overwintering of these delicate plants can quickly add up to a lot of work. The native plant world also offers a variety of beautiful and interesting types that make the use of exotic plants unnecessary.

Planting a New Swimming Pond

The first planting of a swimming pond follows immediately on the construction work. It is often linked directly with filling the pond with water, since many water plants can survive only a short time outside the water. Usually a half hour after drying is sufficient to kill off a sensitive water plant. If there are even brief delays in planting, one must water the plants and cover them with wet cloths to keep them moist.

Planting goes step by step, beginning in the deepest zones of the layout, since one can reach this area only with difficulty after the pond is filled. Deep plant zones are flooded right after setting the plants, even before the shallow zones are planted. Flooding the deep areas in advance is not practical, for so much soil is stirred up in planting that in just a few minutes one can no longer see what one is doing. In addition, the substratum on the slopes would immediately be saturated with water, so that one could no longer walk on these areas without damaging them, It makes sense to have the first planting done by the same company that built the pond. Usually when building begins there is already a plan that includes the subsequent planting. The specialists of the building firm not only know where the appropriate plants go, but usually they can also choose the right point in time to plant the water and shore areas properly.

Setting Plants Carefully

If one does the planting oneself, one should be careful not to use any metal tools if possible, and also to be very careful not to damage the sensitive pond foil. Simple wooden cooking spoons with rounded edges have proved to be practical planting tools. Water and swamp plants with root balls can also be laid on the pond bottom and covered with nutrient-rich soil that one prevents from floating away by adding a few flat stones.

Underwater plants, that just hold onto the bottom with their roots but do not take in any nutrients with them, are anchored to the pond bottom with only a stone as ballast, so they can spread out from there like carpets. Floating plants like water lettuce or water soldiers simply need to be set on the water surface after the swimming pond is flooded.

Substrata

Humus and clay-poor sandy lime soils with silt content, spread some ten centimeters deep on the foil and covered in shore areas with a layer of gravel about four centimeters deep (fine gravel), serve to prevent erosion by waves. A ten-centimeter deep layer of substratum suffices for most root balls. For special cultures such as water lilies, that need a more nutrient-rich and

Left and above: *In the beginning, the freshly planted pond still looks bare, but within a few years luxuriant shore vegetation will develop.*

deeper substratum, regular improvements to the substratum are needed. Or one sets the plants in special plant baskets that are then placed on the pond bottom. A few flat stones paid on top of the pot surface prevent substrata from floating away or rhizomes from floating.

Planting Time

Setting the water plants can be done in the time between spring, as soon as the water is ice-free, and mid-September. Grasses are planted only in the spring months, since they no longer grow in the late summer and autumn. All other plants in containers can be planted during practically all of the season. Not winter-resistant plants should not be planted until mid-May, when no more frosts threaten. When one wants to overwinter them, the right time to take them up is in the autumn—as a rule, early to mid-October—and they are kept, according to their type, in a basin or trough in the house.

Later Additions

Swimming ponds, like all bodies of water, are systems that constantly change. Thus it is not impossible that some plants thrive so well that they become a problem and should be replaced by others. Other plants struggle for some reason and may even die out of the pond's plant community. Whatever happens, there are enough reasons to set new plants into the swimming pond during the year, and it is not always necessary to hire a specialist to do it. Yon can make small changes to the vegetation yourself, as long as you remember a few points:

Plants for a water garden are best bought in spring, and from dependable dealers.

In every planting process, the pond bottom is stirred up and nutrients are released. Thus earth movement should be kept to an absolute minimum. If necessary, plant large quantities of plants at intervals of several days, so that the pond bottom can settle down again in between.

In all work on the pond bottom, one must make sure that the sensitive pond foil is not damaged. Just one sharp-pointed stick can puncture the foil. Once the foil leaks, repairing it is very difficult.

Diseases and damage can be brought in with new plants and influence or even destroy the sensitive balance of the swimming pond. Therefore one should first inspect new plants thoroughly for signs of rot, disease or parasites. One is being very careful when one first keeps new plants in as separate "quarantine basin" for some time and only plants them when one is sure that no unwelcome "guests" are sneaking in.

Unknown plant types that one obtains either as gifts from well-meaning acquaintances or by chance somewhere should not be added to the swimming pond or neighboring vegetation areas in hopes of good luck. It is better to identify them precisely first by using a field guide, and thus learn not only their requirements but also their growing behavior. Thus one avoids unwelcome surprises, such as bringing in wildly growing wild plants.

GOOD TO KNOW

Buying Plants

When you buy water plants, it goes without saying that one should look for high-quality goods. The plants must be stored in clean basins by the dealer, show a good thick growth, and should not show any signs of diseases or parasites. New plants are best bought in mid-spring, shortly before they begin to grow. The plants are sold either with bare roots or in containers. Plants in containers offer the advantage that one immediately obtains large individual plants, but young water plants generally grow well too and have the advantage of being easier to transport. Transporting them is best done in two plastic bags, one inside the other, to prevent water from leaking out. One should make sure that the plants do not get squashed or bent and always remain moist until they are planted. Long distances should be avoided, and so should storing the plants in heat and sunlight.

Since the plants are usually very small when they are planted, pond owners always tend to put in too many plants. As a rule of thumb, four plants are enough for a square meter of regeneration surface. Of the entire mass of plants, 30% should be underwater plants and 70% swamp plants. With water lilies too, one should not overdo it. They spread rapidly and cover up all the underwater plants.

Animals In and Near the Pond

Usually the first guests arrive shortly after planting and flooding. The most direct route is through the air. Water striders are often the pioneers, which sometimes skitter over the water surface after just a few hours. A few days later one can see backswimmers, water beetles and water spiders, and maybe also dragonflies on their exploration flights.

Water snails are often brought in unwillingly with bought or given water plants, which is not necessarily going to hurt the pond. Sometimes resting water birds are the bringers of new pond life. Insect or mollusk eggs stuck in their feathers suddenly mature into new life in the swimming pond. More rarely, amphibians walk in on their own. They settle down in the pond only when a path from the neighborhood leads to a new scene—and when they find sufficient nourishment and housing there. All in all, the supply of food determines whether and how many animals feel at home permanently in and around the pond. Only fish contradict the concept of the self-purifying swimming pond, which many people might regret. But every swimming pond, whether large or small, offers a lot of interesting natural phenomena to observe.

The Smallest Guests: Zooplankton

The guests in the pond that are almost invisible to the naked eye are almost the most important ones: microscopically small creatures (zooplankton). They take nourishment from algae and thus have an important job as water clearers. Because many larger pond dwellers feed in turn on these tiny animals, they form an important link in the food chain of the pond. If they are not brought in along with the water plants, one can "inject" a few liters of water from a healthy pond into the newly-built pond. In one liter of clear pond water there live countless wheel and sun animalculae (scarcely or not at all visible), water fleas *(Vladocera)*, slipper creatures, and hoppers. Since they reproduce unbelievably quickly, it usually does not take long before they have taken over the new swimming pond. But several months pass before, among other things, an ecological balance has been established with their help.

The microscopically small sun-animalculae float freely in sweet water.

Paddle-footed copepods play an important role in the ecological cycle of the swimming pond.

144

Insects

From the air, a body of standing water is easy to recognize from afar. Thus insects are usually the first winged guests at the swimming pond. After the water striders *(Gerris* species) come backswimmers *(Notonecta glauca)*, water spiders and water beetles. Along with the guests, such as butterflies and bees, who only stop briefly on the shore to drink, the pond is also a nursery for many insects. The larvae of the caddisfly *(Sericostoma personatum)* live inconspicuously on the undersides of water-plant leaves or, walled into tiny quivers of sand grains and small stones, on the bottoms of shallow-water zones. Sometimes they may damage water lilies by feeding on them. Collecting them

As dangerous as the big dragonflies look, these flight artists are fully harmless to man.

solves the problem. Other unwanted insects are the water-lily leaf-eater and the water-lily borer, both of which can do much damage to the valuable pond plants.

Numerous other insects populate the shallow-water and regeneration zones of a swimming pond in particular. They feed on algae and plant parts, but many also live as predators and catch smaller pond creatures. Among the insects that are harmless to man but can eat up other pond dwellers in their predatory behavior are the great diving beetle *(Dysticus marginalis),* the grooved beetle *(Acilius),* the tumblebug and the water scorpion bug. Dragonfly larvae are also insatiable predators in the pond. The elegant insects not only prefer to hunt on bodies of water, but also lay their eggs on water plants. From them the brownish-gray larvae emerge and nourish themselves on all the living creatures that come between their jaws in the pond for up to two or three years. They do not even avoid tadpoles. In early summer the elegant flight artists emerge from the wretched-looking larvae. Among the most beautiful are the big darners *(Aeshna)*. Jewelwings *(Calopteryx)* have shimmering colored wings and fly soundlessly over the pond. The rather husky skimmers *(Libellula)* are more often found by flowing waters.

Gnats

The swimming pond is an ideal nursery for all kinds of gnats. Along with some that are harmless to people, such as midges *(Chironomus)* and phantom midges *(Chaoboridae)*, the blood-sucking mosquitoes *(Culex, Aedes* and *Anopheles)* also creed there. In water warmed by the sun, the transparent, glassy larvae need only a few days to develop before the flying adult insect emerges. From early summer to early autumn, one generation succeeds the last. One would suspect that a plague of mosquitoes would break out wherever there is standing water. This is not true, for numerous small creatures, especially water insects and amphibians, feed on the gnat larvae. Where the ecological balance more or less applies and there are enough enemies to eat them, mosquitoes do not have a chance. In rain barrels and birdbaths, on the other hand, where there are scarcely any enemies to eat them, the blood-sucking creatures develop practically undisturbed. A study made by Biotop Landschaftsgestaltung GmbH has shown that mosquitoes are one of the three main concerns of people who are thinking of building a pond. But if one asks pond owners af-

Mosquito larvae live in sweet water. They often become the prey of larger insect larvae, which is why a swimming pond does not have a plague of mosquitoes.

ter the first year, they say that mosquitoes were not a problem for them, and all their skepticism has vanished.

Water Snails

Water snails have an important job to do in their living space. Unlike the voracious snails in ornamental and practical gardens, they are not regarded as a plague, for they wipe out the annoying thread algae and eat dead plant parts. In summer one finds their gall-like egg cases on the undersides of water-lily leaves and those of other water plants. Many water snails *(Lymnaea, Radix* or *Stagnicola)* can transmit cercariae, major parasites that cause the unpleasant cercarial dermatitis, especially in the early summer. In this case all snails must be gathered and removed from the pond. But the prime hosts of cercariae are water birds.

Where water snails do not occur on their own or in sufficient variety, one can help the cause: Special garden shops for water gardens usually offer various kinds of them. The great pond snail *(Lymnaea stagnalis)* grows to some six centimeters in length, has a pointed shell and stays on the water surface. The plate snail *(Planorbis planorbis)* has a round, flat shell. Similar but somewhat larger is the posthorn snail *(Planorbarius corneus)*. Its characteristic dark to reddish brown shell reaches a diameter of up to three centimeters. The swamp snail

(Viviparus viviparous), somewhat reminiscent of vineyard snails, gives birth to live young instead of laying eggs. Thus it does not increase as quickly as other kinds of water snails.

Pond mussels *(Anodonta)* can also live well in a swimming pond. Even though man does not see much of them, they help to keep the water clean. With the help of an extended foot, they creep over the bottom and thus filter the water. The filtering capacity of an adult mussel is said to reach 1000 liters of pond water per day.

Amphibians

The presence of frogs is usually regarded as a clear indication that a pond is functioning "naturally". In fact, frogs, toads and tailed amphibians come only when they find good homes and plenty of food in the pond and its surroundings. For the functioning of a swimming pond, amphibians and not necessarily needed. But where they immigrate, all the native kinds fit into the natural food chain of the swimming pond. They eat insects, snails and their eggs, and thus keep their numbers in bounds. The tadpoles and other young amphibians in turn serve as food for other pond dwellers such as dragonfly and beetle larvae.

The brown grass frog *(Rana temporaria)* and the rare green leaf frog *(Hyla arborea)* come to the water only to spawn. The green water frog types *(Rana esculenta, R. lessonare*

147

Post-horn snails are easy to identify by their characteristic shells.

and *R. ridibunda)* live in the pond all year. Less noticeable than the frogs, which are active by day are the toads, which only come out of their burrows at night. One encounters the common European toad *(Bufo bufo)* most often. Among their prey are insects as well as night snails. Other types of toads, or the related speckled toads *(Bombina)*, are rarer. The toads seek the pond mainly in the spring as a place to spawn. The gall-like eggs resemble those of the frogs but are not found in large clumps, but rather in long strands between water plants. Salamanders *(Triturus),* also known as newts, also look for standing bodies of water at spawning time. The native varieties are often visitors to the swimming area as well, where they hunt zooplankton. Usually they arrive in pairs. One can recognize the males by the ridges on their backs. Because of their curiosity, salamanders are easy to catch and observe closely. But they feel better if one leaves them alone.

Swimming Among Frogs

Imagining that while you were swimming, frogs, salamanders or other slippery amphibians suddenly got in your way is ungrounded. Before the swimming season begins in June, most amphibians have left the pond, which they used only to spawn. Besides, these animals prefer to be in the shallow-water zone of the regeneration area, where they can hide and find food among the plants. The swimming area does not interest them, since the water there contains no nourishment.

Waiting or Helping?

Even if the temptation to upgrade your own biotope with frogs and salamanders from natural bodies of water is so great, amphibians, their larvae or eggs, are never allowed to be taken from their natural habitat to put them in one's own swimming pond. This is contrary to nature protection laws and also very rarely succeeds. Usually the transferred animals go away after a short time and, in the worst cases, lose their lives on some road on the way back to their ancestral home.

When Frogs Croak

If you have been lucky enough to have amphibians settle in your swimming pond after all, it can become an annoyance despite all your joy. The nightly croaking of frogs at mating time can reach a volume that prevents quiet sleep, even with the windows closed. In particular, neighbors who do not share the practical advantages of a swimming pond soon feel disturbed by it. Complaints do not help in such a case, for the frogs do not let their croaking be silenced—and since they cannot be removed from either natural bodies of water but also artificial ones according to nature protection laws, they cannot be gotten rid of. As a solution to this dilemma, German courts suggests requesting a permit to remove (resettle) the frogs from the nature protection officials of your state or county. In principle, though, one should ask oneself whether the sounds of nature—be they frogs croaking or birds twittering—are not in any case more bearable than automobile or aircraft noise, or the constant noise from building sites, motor-driven apparatus used in home or garden care.

Reptiles

Although the water is not their real habitat, many reptiles occur at more or less natural bodies of water. The ring snake *(Natter natter)*, not poisonous or harmful to man, is easy to recognize by the yellow spots on each side of the back of its head. In the water it hunts tadpoles, swamp turtles, and other interesting pond dwellers that particularly fascinate children. But since they, like fish, pollute the water strongly with their droppings, they should not be allowed in the swimming pond.

Fish in the Swimming Pond

Whoever thinks about animals in the water naturally thinks first of fish. Especially for children, tame goldfish that they can feed and watch from the shore are a great attraction. But fish have no business being in a swimming pond. This has various reasons: Young fish feed mainly on zooplankton, which means the fish eat up the "filter system" of the swimming pond. They also enrich the water with nutrients from their droppings. If they are also fed, a further troublesome component is added, for the part of the food that is not eaten fertilizes the pond flowers. Then algae eat the released nutrients and becloud the water by their massive reproduction.

Along with the harmful influences that the metabolism of the fish have on the water quality, many fish are also predators. Even small types

Among the salamanders that turn up in the pond at mating time, the males are especially strikingly colored.

As interesting as fish are, like these sticklebacks, they have no business in a swimming pond.

like sticklebacks eat a great many water fleas, which are then not present to reduce algae. Although they also eat mosquito larvae, tadpoles and many insect larvae, like those of dragonflies, are also eaten by predatory fish. The satiation is very simple: without larvae and tadpoles, there are no dragonflies and no frogs. Thus even a small fish population can quickly become a problem for the other pond dwellers and lead to a shortage of species—just the opposite of what one wanted from the introduction of fish.

Native Types

Many people may think that it cannot be so bad to put in small numbers of very small fish—and that native species like sticklebacks, moderlieschen, yellowwort and minnows are well suited to life in small bodies of water. But a few specimens very quickly, in a very natural way, become many—and they can do a lot of damage to the sensible management of a swimming pond.

As for native fish in a swimming pond, there are all kinds of opinions. Some experts take the position that in very large ponds small numbers of small native fish can be tolerated. In case of doubt, everyone must decide for himself. Whoever wants to put fish in a swimming pond should give the water one or two years after the pond was built, so that the plants can grow and a microfauna and –flora can develop that allow the fish to survive. But even in such big ponds, on must avoid large and lively species like goldfish, carp, or even koi. In no case should they be put in a swimming pond. The clearing function of the water plants is not sufficient to neutralize their droppings. In addition, they tend to stir up the pond bottom. They uproot and ruin the underwater plants, and soon the rhizome of, for example, a beloved water lily is driven to the water surface.

Check List: Annual Care

The great advantage of swimming ponds is the relative ease of maintaining them. Unlike tiled pools, swimming ponds do not have to be cleaned regularly of blown-in leaves, and algae on the walls are no reason for hectic action. In the first year one can limit oneself practically to enjoying the water. Only when the strings of algae take the upper hand must one fish them out occasionally with a net.

Regularly cutting back the water and shore-zone plants is a part of pond care.

Spring Care

When the ice melts, dead stalks of cattails and other water plants can be cut off and, along with other dead plant parts, taken out of the pond.

During cleaning and thinning work, one should watch out for resting amphibians and laid eggs.

Before the swimming season begins, the layer of mud on the swimming area should be removed with a mud-sucker.

Summer Care

Strand algae should be removed if there are too many of them.

Floating plants like water lilies, frogbit and water lettuce can increase very much. Removing part of the plants now and then takes nutrients out of the swimming pond and contributes to keeping the water pure.

Spreading underwater plants in all zones of the pond can be cut back every two months to take nutrients out of the swimming pond. The plants must not be pulled out. Cut material can be composted. In areas that are not readily available, cutting can be done from an air mattress.

Warming of the water encourages algae growth. Swimming ponds in sunny places should then be partially shaded with a sunshade or awning.

If there is a lot of humus on the bottom of the swimming zone during the swimming season, it must be removed regularly with the mod-sucker.

Water must be refilled if there is a lot of evaporation in long dry spells.

Autumn Care

After a few years the swimming pond begins to be filled in around the edges. Early autumn is the best time to reduce the plant cover in the shore zone somewhat. It is best to do this to a different part of the shore every year, so as not to disturb all the microflora and –fauna.

If the shallow-water area starts to become filled in, some of the pond water should be pumped out and the dirt removed from the shore zones.

Autumn leaves bring too many nutrients into the water. If there are broadleaf trees in the vicinity and their leaves are blown into the pond, one can cover the swimming pond with a net, A net can be put in place more easily if cords are stretched across the swimming pond.

Winter Care

Dry stalks of cattails, rushes and other plants should not be cut off right away. They allow a gas exchange with the swimming pond is frozen and prevent the pond fauna from being suffocated by harmful gases.

Before the pond freezes is the right time to put an ice vent (a styropore ring or similar device available in the trade) into the pond. This enables harmful gases to escape from the pond and fresh air to enter it.

The ice cover should never be cut up. The amphibians and other small animals hibernating in the shore area will suffer from it.

With a long-handled net one can remove leaves and other material from the water.

Resources

Organizations

**Deutsche Gesellschaft fuer naturnahe Bade-
gewaesser e. V. (DGfnB)**
Bei der Ratsmuehle 14
D-21355 Lueneburg
Phone 07000/7008787
www.kleinbadeteiche.de

**Verband Oesterreichischer Schwimmteich-
bauer (VO"S)**
www.schwimmteich,co.at
email: verband.oe.schwimmteichbauer@gmx.at

**Schweizerischer Verband naturnaher Badege-
waesser und Pflanzwenklaeranlagen (SVBP)**
Im Schoerli 3
CH-8600 Duebendorf
Phone: +41 (0)1 835 78 08
Fax +41 (0)1 835 78 79
www.svbp.org

Pond-building Firms

Biotop Landschaftsgestaltung GmbH
Hauptstrasse 285
A-3411 Weidling
Phone +43 (0)2243-304 06-13
Fax +43 (0)2243-304 06-22
www.swimming-teich.com

Bohr und das Gruen
Kohlenbrucher Weg
D-66663 Merzig-Schwemlingen
Phone 06861-75165
Fax 06861-74609
www.bohr-baumschule.de

**Bahl Garten-, Landschafts- und Schwimmte-
ichbau**
Hauptstrasse 48
D-25368 Kiebitzreihe/Elmshorn
Phone 04121-5900
Fax 04121-50356
www.bahlgalabau.de

Daldrup Garten- und Landschaftsbau
Burg Huelshoff
Schonebeck 6
D-48329 Havixbeck
Phone 02534-64670
Fax 02534-646729
www.daldrup.de

Egli Gartenbau AG
Curtibergstrasse 21
CH-8646 Wagen SG
Phone +41 (0) 55-212 33 83
Fax +41 (0) 55-212 54 83
www.egliwagen.ch

Fuchs baut Gaerten GmbH
Schlegldorf 91 A
D-83661 Lenggries
Phone 08042-914 54 0
Fax 08042-914 54 22
www.fuchs-baut-gaerten.de

**Helmut Haas GmbH & Co. KG Garten-. Land-
schafts- und Sportplatzbau**
Hochbergweg 4
D-88239 Wangen-Roggenzell
Phone 07528-958 0
Fax 07528-958 30
www.haas-galabau.de

Garten- und Landschaftsbau Pohl GmbH
Bayerwald Baumschule
Ziefling-Bierl 2
D-93497 Willmering
Phone 09971-84590
Fax 09971-845950
www.gartenbau-pohl.de

**Erlebnisgarten Schleitzer GmbH Garten- und
Landschaftsbau**
Enterstrasse 23
D-80999 Muenchen
Phone 089-89 28 65 0
Fax 089-89 28 65 50
www.schleitzer.de

Periodicals

Der Schwimmteich
Herausgegeben von der Deutschen Gesellschaft fuer naturnahe Badegewaesser (DGfnB e.V.), dem Verband oesterreichischer Schwimmteichbauer (VO"S) und dem schweizerischen Verband naturnaher Badegewaesser und Pflanzenklaeranlagen (SVBP), erscheint vier Mal jaehrlich im Verlag Agrimedia GmbH,
Spithal 4, D-29468 Bergen/Dumme
Phone 05845/988110
www.schwimmteich-magazin.com

Gartenteich—Das Wassergarten-magazin
Erscheint sechs Mal jaehrlich im Daehne Verlag GmbH
Am Erlengraben 8, D-76275 Ettlingen
Phone 07243/575-0
www.gartenteich.com

Eden—Das Magazin fuer Gartengestaltung
Erscheint vierteljaehrlich bei der medienfabrik Guietersloh GmbH
Carl-Bertelsmann-Strasse 33, D-33311 Guetersloh
Phone 05241/23480-10
www.eden-magazin.de

Books

Barth, Ulrsula, Christa Brand & Nik Barlo, Jr., *Teiche und Badeteiche*, Munich, Callwey, 2000.

Dobler, Anna, and Wolfgang Fleischer, *Der Schwimmteich im Garten*, Vienna, Orac, 1999.

Franke, Wolfram, *Der Traum vom eigenen Schwimmteich*, Munich, BLV, 1999.

Himlelhuiber, Peter, *Das Wassergarten-Baunuch*, Munich, Callwey, 2004. English version, *Watergardens*, Schiffer Publishing: Atglen, 2007.

Love, Gilly, *Wasser im Garten*, Munich, Callwey, 2002.

Neuenschwander, Eduard, *Schwimmteiche*, Stuttgart, Ulmer, 2000.

Robinson, Peter, *Traumhafte Wassergaerten*, Augsburg, Augustus, 2001.

Rohlfing, Ines Maria and Mehdi, Mahabadi, *Schwimm- und Badeteichanlagen*, Stuttgart, Ulmer, 2005.

Wachter, Karl, *Der Wassergarten*, Stuttgart, Ulmer, 2005.

Weixler, Richard and Hauer, Wolfgang, *Garten- und Schwimmteiche*, Graz, Stocker, 2003

Index